Hidden Networks

Dr. Horen Kuecuekyan

Technics Publications
SEDONA, ARIZONA

⫿⫿ TECHNICS PUBLICATIONS

115 Linda Vista, Sedona, AZ 86336 USA
https://www.TechnicsPub.com

Edited by Steve Hoberman
Cover design by Lorena Molinari

First Printing 2025

Copyright © 2025 by Dr. Horen Kuecuekyan

ISBN, print ed.   9781634628181
ISBN, Kindle ed.   9781634628211
ISBN, PDF ed.   9781634628723

Library of Congress Control Number: 2025939861

Contents

Unveiling the Invisible

In an era characterized by the seamless flow of data across continents, devices, and human interactions, the capacity to discern patterns has transcended the realm of art to become a precise scientific discipline. Over the past several decades, the practice of data collection has undergone a profound transformation. Initially confined to rudimentary manual recording techniques, it has since progressed to sophisticated digital systems capable of amassing vast quantities of information in real-time. While this evolution has revolutionized research and decision-making, it has also been accompanied by progressively intricate challenges, particularly in environments characterized by hostility.

This book extends the methodologies discussed in "Data Collection in Hostile Environments" to address a more complex and potentially extensive challenge: identifying and analyzing coordinated group movements that traverse seemingly disparate networks yet converge toward shared objectives.

These "network movements" represent one of the most sophisticated phenomena in our increasingly interconnected global environment, where causality is elusive, attribution is challenging, and conventional analytical frameworks frequently fail to capture the full dimensionality of coordinated action.

The Evolution of Network Analysis

The digital transformation has fundamentally reshaped the formation, communication, and behavior of networks. Physical proximity, verbal coordination, and visible leadership, once prerequisites for effective collaboration, have evolved into decentralized structures operating through encrypted channels. These structures employ algorithmic coordination and artificial intelligence to optimize their activities. While conventional analytical tools may perceive these networks as independent actors, they function with remarkable synchronicity when analyzed through specialized lenses.

Quantum computing has revolutionized our ability to process multidimensional network relationships, which were once computationally infeasible. Neuromorphic computing architectures, drawing inspiration from the intricate neural networks of the human brain, have facilitated the identification of patterns that mimic human recognition capabilities while operating at a scale comparable to machines. Furthermore, synthetic biology techniques have introduced computational frameworks inspired by collective biological systems, such as ant colonies or microbiome communities, providing novel avenues for comprehending emergent network behaviors.

The Challenge of Modern Network Movements

Today's network movements exhibit several defining characteristics that distinguish them from conventional organizational structures:

- Decision-making authorities are dispersed across multiple nodes, providing resilience against targeted disruption and obscuring centralized control.

- Actions appear coordinated despite minimal direct communication, implying sophisticated timing mechanisms or shared algorithmic directives.

- Networks rapidly reorganize in response to external pressures, shedding compromised nodes while maintaining operational continuity.

- The ability to rapidly convert one form of resource (financial, informational, reputational) into another, fostering flexibility and resilience.

- The capability to generate activity patterns that resemble natural, uncoordinated behaviors, effectively concealing intentional coordination.

Due to these characteristics, traditional analytical approaches have become increasingly impractical. Standard network analysis tools primarily concentrate on static relationships rather than dynamic patterns that emerge over time and across multiple dimensions. Statistical methods, based on the assumption of independence, encounter difficulties when applied to intentionally interdependent systems designed to conceal their connections.

A New Analytical Paradigm

This comprehensive methodology presents a novel approach to analyzing intricate network movements across diverse domains. Based on advancements in quantum information theory, topological data analysis, and computational neuroscience, we introduce frameworks that surpass conventional analytical constraints.

Our approach integrates several cutting-edge technologies:

- **Federated Learning Systems** that can identify patterns across distributed datasets without centralizing potentially sensitive information, which is crucial when analyzing networks that span jurisdictional and organizational boundaries.

- **Quantum Tensor Networks** offer mathematical frameworks for modeling high-dimensional relationships that classical computational models cannot adequately capture.

- **Biomimetic Algorithms** are inspired by natural systems demonstrating emergent coordination, such as murmuration patterns in starling flocks or collective decision-making in microbiological communities.

- **Temporal Graph Neural Networks** can track relationship evolution across time while identifying causality patterns that may be temporally displaced or intentionally obscured.

- **Synthetic Data Augmentation** techniques that enable hypothesis testing against counterfactual scenarios, allowing analysts to distinguish between coordinated action and coincidental alignment.

Ethical Considerations and Democratic Governance

The methodologies presented in this book possess considerable power, a power that necessitates ethical governance and democratic oversight. Authoritarian regimes could exploit the capacity to discern concealed network movements to suppress legitimate civil society activities with equal ease as they could utilize it to identify nefarious influence operations posing threats to democratic institutions.

Consequently, we devote substantial attention to the ethical frameworks necessary for the responsible deployment of these analytical techniques. These encompass robust anonymization protocols, transparent oversight mechanisms, adversarial fairness testing, and clearly defined application contexts.

The Road Ahead

The following chapters will guide readers through increasingly sophisticated analytical techniques, beginning with fundamental pattern recognition and progressing toward advanced implementations of quantum-enhanced topological analysis for multi-dimensional network movements.

Each methodology is presented with practical implementation guidelines, computational requirements, validation frameworks, and case studies drawn from real-world applications and appropriately anonymized and abstracted to protect operational security while preserving instructional value.

By the conclusion of this book, readers will possess both the theoretical understanding and practical tools necessary to identify, analyze, and comprehend complex network movements operating across multiple domains. In doing so, they will gain insight into one of the defining phenomena of our interconnected age. How does distributed agency coalesce into coordinated action, often invisible to conventional analysis yet profoundly influential in shaping our world?

In an era where the most consequential forces often operate beyond the threshold of obvious visibility, these capabilities represent not merely academic interest but essential tools for understanding the evolving dynamics of power, influence, and collective action in the twenty-first century.

CHAPTER 1

The Symphony of Independent Actors

Imagine standing at the edge of a bustling marketplace. Hundreds of individuals move about with purpose, each pursuing their own objectives. Vendors arrange their wares, shoppers browse with varying degrees of intent, couriers navigate through crowds delivering packages, and discreet exchanges of information, goods, and currency occur continuously amidst it all. At first glance, this scene appears chaotic, a cacophony of individual actions without coherence. However, upon closer observation, patterns emerge. The marketplace functions as a unified entity, serving its overarching purpose despite the absence of a central conductor orchestrating each participant's movements.

This marketplace exemplifies a "multi-agent system," a collection of independent entities operating simultaneously with distinct objectives, yet collectively contributing to a broader systemic function. Analyzing such systems presents one of the most challenging tasks in contemporary analysis across diverse domains.

The complexity arises from the inherent interplay among actors. While individual behaviors may appear straightforward or even predictable, the emergence of collective behaviors and patterns when these actors interact with their environment becomes evident. This phenomenon is akin to attempting to comprehend a symphony by studying individual musical notes rather than listening to the orchestrated whole.

Traditional analytical approaches often prove ineffective in addressing complex systems.

These approaches typically employ reductionist methods, dividing intricate phenomena into constituent components and studying each in isolation before reconstructing comprehension. While this approach has demonstrated value in various scientific and analytical settings, it becomes inadequate when interactions between components fundamentally alter the system's behavior.

Our objective in this book is to establish a comprehensive methodological framework for analyzing these concealed networks of independent actors, a framework that acknowledges both individual agency and systemic emergence. We will explore how seemingly disparate entities can form cohesive systems with discernible patterns and predictable outcomes despite the absence of centralized control.

Financial Markets, Healthcare, Criminal Networks

The principles and methodologies we explore transcend academic curiosity and have profound practical applications across diverse domains where intricate multi-agent systems naturally emerge.

Consider financial markets, where thousands of traders execute millions of transactions daily. Each trader operates independently, adhering to their own strategy and responding to various signals while pursuing individual profit objectives. However, collectively, these actions generate market trends, determine asset prices, and distribute capital throughout the global economy. Comprehending how these individual decisions aggregate into market movements facilitates more effective investment strategies, establishes improved regulatory frameworks, and enhances financial stability.

Within healthcare systems, a diverse array of stakeholders interact within a complex ecosystem, including hospitals, patients, insurers, pharmaceutical companies, and regulatory bodies. Each entity has distinct objectives: hospitals prioritize providing quality care while ensuring financial sustainability, patients seek access to effective treatment at affordable costs, insurers manage risk pools across diverse populations, and pharmaceutical companies focus on developing medications while seeking returns on research investments. The interactions between these stakeholders shape healthcare outcomes, costs, and accessibility. We can identify intervention points by charting these relationships to enhance system-wide efficiency and improve patient outcomes.

Notably, criminal and terrorist networks function as clandestine systems of independent actors meticulously crafted to evade detection. Despite their absence of formal hierarchies, these networks demonstrate sophisticated organizational structures. Comprehending the flow of information, resources, and directives through these clandestine networks is paramount for law enforcement and security agencies. Authorities can more effectively disrupt illicit activities by pinpointing key nodes, communication channels, and operational patterns.

The versatility of our analytical framework becomes evident when applied to these diverse domains. The same fundamental principles elucidating market fluctuations can illuminate patient care pathways or reveal vulnerabilities in terrorist financing networks. This cross-domain applicability is one of the framework's most valuable attributes, with its capacity to derive insights from seemingly disparate systems by recognizing their shared structural and behavioral characteristics.

A Holistic Analytical Approach

Traditional methodologies for comprehending intricate systems have predominantly employed domain-specific approaches. Financial analysts have developed specialized tools for market dynamics that differ significantly from those utilized by healthcare administrators or intelligence analysts. While these specialized approaches provide depth within their respective domains, they frequently overlook opportunities to cross-pollinate ideas and techniques.

We aspire to establish a domain-neutral framework, a collection of applicable analytical principles and methodologies irrespective of the specific system being scrutinized. This holistic approach presents several distinct advantages.

First, it facilitates knowledge transfer across traditionally siloed domains. Insights gained from studying financial market dynamics can inform our understanding of social network formation. Techniques developed to analyze healthcare systems can illuminate patterns in criminal organizations. This cross-disciplinary fertilization often yields breakthrough insights that remain undiscovered within domain boundaries.

Second, a holistic approach facilitates the identification of universal principles governing complex multi-agent systems. Despite surface-level differences, many systems exhibit similar structural properties and behavioral patterns. By abstracting away domain-specific details, we can identify these universal characteristics and develop generalized theories with broader explanatory power.

Third, it promotes methodological innovation. When analysts from different domains collaborate using a common framework, they bring diverse perspectives to shared analytical challenges. This diversity of thought catalyzes creative problem-solving and methodological advancement that benefits all domains simultaneously.

Nevertheless, developing such a framework necessitates meticulous consideration of competing priorities. It must be sufficiently comprehensive to capture fundamental system dynamics across diverse contexts while maintaining flexibility to accommodate domain-specific intricacies. It must provide ample analytical power without becoming excessively complex, obfuscating rather than illuminating. Throughout this book, we will strive to harmonize these considerations, aiming for a framework that balances potency and practicality.

Dynamic Adaptability vs. Static Frameworks

Many analytical frameworks suffer from a critical limitation: their static nature. They offer only snapshot views of systems at specific moments, neglecting to account for their temporal evolution. This limitation becomes particularly pertinent when analyzing multi-agent systems, which are inherently dynamic and continuously adapt to changing circumstances and internal developments.

Our approach prioritizes dynamic adaptability, enabling the evolution of analytical models in response to evolving system behaviors. Instead of generating fixed representations that quickly become obsolete, we develop methodologies incorporating feedback loops that facilitate continuous refinement as new data becomes available and system conditions fluctuate.

This dynamic perspective acknowledges several fundamental realities of complex systems:

- Complex systems rarely remain static; they undergo evolution through internal adaptation mechanisms, external influences, and random fluctuations. An effective analytical framework must capture this evolutionary trajectory, not merely present static states.

- Individual actors within systems often acquire knowledge through experience, modifying their behaviors based on outcomes and observations. These learning processes can fundamentally alter system dynamics over time.

- External environments undergo transformations, altering the operational conditions of systems. Economic policies undergo shifts, novel technologies emerge, and social norms evolve and all potentially triggering cascading changes throughout interconnected systems.

- When analysts or authorities intervene in systems based on initial observations, the systems often adapt in response, sometimes neutralizing or circumventing the intervention. This dynamic necessitates analytical frameworks capable of predicting and accounting for these adaptive responses.

To address these challenges, our methodology incorporates several key features, starting with:

- Temporal analysis of system properties and behaviors over various time scales.

- Explicitly representing how agents and systems respond to changing conditions is presented with adaptation modeling.

- Scenario simulation is used to test potential future states under various conditions and interventions.

- Regularly comparing model predictions against emerging real-world data happens with continuous validation.

- Rapid adjustment of model parameters is necessary as new information emerges; flexible parametrization is the process.

By adopting this dynamic perspective, our framework remains pertinent even as the systems under investigation evolve. It transforms analysis from a static snapshot into an ongoing dialogue between models and reality, continuously refining comprehension as systems change.

Throughout this book, we will revisit the metaphor of a symphony to elucidate the relationship between individual actors and systemic wholes. This metaphor provides rich parallels to the intricate systems we endeavor to comprehend.

In a symphony orchestra, numerous musicians play distinct instruments, each adhering to their own musical line. Each musician primarily focuses on their individual contribution. Yet, from this collection of concentrated individual efforts, a cohesive musical experience emerges as a symphony that transcends any single instrumental part.

Several aspects of this metaphor warrant further elaboration. Within an orchestra, instruments perform distinct functions. Similarly, within intricate systems, diverse types of agents assume specialized roles that mutually complement one another. While a conductor provides general guidance, they do not exert direct control over each musician's individual actions. Musicians rely on peripheral awareness of their peers, responsive adjustments, and shared comprehension of the musical score.

In numerous complex systems, coordination emerges through analogous mechanisms rather than centralized control.

Musical compositions unfold over time, with themes evolving, recurring, and undergoing transformations. The symphony metaphor serves not merely as a poetic embellishment but as a genuine analytical lens. By conceptualizing complex systems as symphonic compositions, we shift our perspective from reductionist to holistic, from static to dynamic, from mechanistic to organic. This transformation facilitates the acquisition of insights that might otherwise remain elusive.

As we progress through subsequent chapters, we construct our methodological framework incrementally. With this holistic perspective in mind, it will elucidate the intricate relationships between microscopic behaviors and macroscopic patterns, between individual agency and collective emergence, and between apparent chaos and underlying order.

In this chapter, we have established the foundational challenge: comprehending systems composed of independent actors pursuing individual objectives while collectively contributing to overarching functions. We have acknowledged the limitations of conventional analytical approaches and advocated for a holistic, dynamically adaptable framework applicable across diverse domains.

The subsequent chapters will systematically develop this framework, progressing from theoretical foundations to practical methodologies. We will explore data acquisition strategies, behavioral fingerprinting techniques, agent-based modeling approaches, game-theoretic analyses, network visualization methods, and the application of Large Language Models (LLMs) for interpretation. Throughout, we will maintain our commitment to cross-domain applicability, dynamic adaptability, and the equilibrium between analytical power and practical utility.

We commence with the fundamental components of our framework, the methodologies employed for identifying, characterizing, and modeling the subgroups that constitute intricate systems. We will delve into hierarchical modeling techniques that facilitate the mapping of the boundaries, objectives, and actions of these subgroups, thereby establishing architectural comprehension upon which all subsequent analysis will be predicated.

CHAPTER 2

Hierarchical Modeling of Complex Systems

To comprehend a complex system of independent actors, it is essential to establish a systematic approach to identifying and characterizing the subgroups that constitute it. These subgroups are collections of actors that share specific attributes, behaviors, or objectives that differentiate them from other elements within the system. The identification process is both an art and a science, necessitating a fusion of domain expertise and analytical rigor.

The first challenge lies in determining the appropriate criteria for delineating subgroups:

- **Behavioral patterns**: Actors exhibiting similar behavioral signatures can be naturally categorized. For instance, in financial markets, traders can be classified based on their trading frequencies, risk tolerances, or preferred asset classes. Similarly, in social networks, individuals can be clustered based on their communication patterns, content sharing behaviors, or engagement metrics.

- **Functional roles**: Actors performing analogous functions within a system frequently constitute cohesive subgroups. Within healthcare systems, we can differentiate between primary care providers, specialists, emergency services, administrative staff, and patients each representing a functionally distinct subgroup with distinct operational dynamics.

- **Objective alignment**: Actors pursuing similar objectives naturally form subgroups. In political systems, individuals with shared ideological orientations establish parties or movements. In criminal networks, those specializing in specific illicit activities (e.g., money laundering, smuggling, cybercrime) constitute functional subgroups.

- **Structural position**: An actor's position within the overall network topology determines subgroup membership. Actors who serve as bridges between otherwise disconnected network segments form a structurally significant subgroup regardless of their individual attributes or behaviors.

- **Temporal synchronization**: Actors operating in similar timeframes or whose activities exhibit temporal correlation can be temporally defined subgroups. This criterion is particularly relevant in systems with cyclical patterns or distinct operational phases.

The identification process typically commences with exploratory data analysis, employing visualization techniques and descriptive statistics to discern apparent patterns. This initial exploration serves as a foundation for selecting more sophisticated analytical methods, such as cluster analysis, community detection algorithms, and latent variable models, which can unveil non-evident groupings.

It is crucial to recognize that subgroup boundaries are rarely definitive. The majority of intricate systems exhibit graded memberships, with certain actors firmly positioned within specific subgroups while others occupy boundary positions or maintain affiliations with multiple subgroups simultaneously. Our analytical approach must accommodate this ambiguous boundary reality rather than imposing arbitrarily sharp delineations that oversimplify system complexity.

Furthermore, subgroups are rarely static; they undergo evolution over time as system conditions fluctuate, individual actors adapt, and interactions reshape relationships. Consequently, effective characterization must encompass temporal dimensions, thereby tracking how subgroup compositions, behaviors, and roles transform throughout system evolution.

Mapping Boundaries and Understanding Objectives

Once we have identified the relevant subgroups within a system, we must delve deeper to map their boundaries with precision and comprehend their specific objectives. This comprehensive mapping serves as the foundation for subsequent analysis of interactions and emergent behaviors.

Boundary mapping necessitates a multi-dimensional approach. Physical boundaries define spatial domains within which subgroups operate in geographical territories, jurisdictional regions, or virtual spaces. Functional boundaries delineate the range of activities and responsibilities assigned to or assumed by specific subgroups. Informational boundaries determine what knowledge is accessible to subgroup members versus what remains external to their awareness. Social boundaries establish who is a member of the subgroup, who remains outside, and what levels of permeability exist for new entrants or departing members.

These boundaries rarely align precisely. A subgroup may maintain stringent informational boundaries while operating across vast geographical territories, or it may occupy a narrowly defined functional niche while maintaining highly permeable social boundaries.

The interplay between these diverse boundary types frequently generates tensions that drive system dynamics and evolution.

To effectively understand subgroup objectives, a comprehensive approach that extends beyond stated goals to examine revealed preferences through actual behaviors is necessary. Stated objectives, which are explicitly articulated by subgroup members or formal documentation, provide initial insights but may reflect aspirational intentions rather than operational realities. Revealed objectives, discernible through observed behaviors and resource allocations, often offer more reliable indicators of actual priorities.

Objectives typically exist in hierarchies, with high-level goals decomposing into subordinate objectives that guide specific actions. These hierarchies can be systematically mapped through techniques such as goal decomposition analysis, which breaks down overarching objectives into progressively more specific sub-goals until reaching actionable directives.

Objectives rarely operate independently; they interact through complementarity, competition, or conditional relationships.

Complementary objectives mutually reinforce one another, progressing toward one, while simultaneously advancing others. Competitive objectives introduce trade-offs, where advancing one inevitably impedes others. Conditional objectives establish dependencies, where certain goals must be accomplished before others become viable.

Configuring these objective relationships within and between subgroups provides critical insights into system dynamics. Areas of objective alignment present opportunities for collaboration and synergy, while points of objective conflict generate tensions that may drive competition, negotiation, or innovation.

> By meticulously mapping both boundaries and objectives, we establish the foundational understanding upon which more advanced analysis can be built. This mapping must be periodically revisited and refined as systems evolve, and new data becomes available.

Constructing Hierarchical Models

With the identification and characterization of subgroups, we can now construct hierarchical models that depict the structural organization of intricate systems. These models not only encompass the components themselves, but also the interrelationships between them across various levels of aggregation.

Hierarchical modeling offers several analytical advantages. By structuring system elements into nested levels of abstraction, hierarchical models render complexity manageable, enabling analysts to concentrate on specific levels or components without succumbing to the overwhelming complexity of the system's entirety. Within intricate systems, various phenomena often manifest at distinct scales. Hierarchical models facilitate the simultaneous examination of micro-level interactions, meso-level subgroup dynamics, and macro-level system behaviors.

Hierarchical structures optimize information processing by filtering and aggregating data as it traverses levels, thereby reducing noise and emphasizing salient patterns. Hierarchical organization facilitates system adaptation by enabling modifications to occur within specific components or levels without necessarily disrupting the entire structure.

The construction of hierarchical models commences by determining the appropriate number of levels. While this varies depending on system complexity, most analyses benefit from incorporating at least three tiers: the micro-level, encompassing individual actors and their immediate interactions; the meso-level, which focuses on subgroups and their internal dynamics; and the macro-level, which analyzes system-wide patterns and emergent behaviors.

More intricate systems may necessitate additional intermediate levels to effectively capture sub-subgroups, coalitions, or other structural components.

For each identified level, we delineate the constituent elements (the entities present at that level), compositional relationships (how elements at that level are composed or are composed of elements at adjacent levels), horizontal interactions (the way elements at that level interact with one another), and vertical influences (the way elements at that level influence or are influenced by elements at adjacent levels).

These specifications can be represented through various formalisms. Hierarchical network models provide graph-based representations where nodes and edges exist at multiple levels, with meta-nodes representing aggregations of lower-level components. Nested agent-based models offer simulation frameworks where agents exist within nested environments, with higher-level behaviors emerging from lower-level interactions. Multi-level statistical models present analytical approaches that explicitly model variance and covariance structures across different hierarchical levels.

Appropriate modeling formalisms are selected based on analytical objectives, data accessibility, and computational limitations. Frequently, complementary models employing distinct formalisms yield the most comprehension, as each captures aspects of system structure that others may overlook.

Hierarchical models must strike a balance between fidelity and parsimony.

They must capture fundamental structural characteristics while avoiding superfluous complexity that could obscure rather than illuminate system understanding. This equilibrium typically emerges through iterative refinement, with initial models subjected to validation against empirical data and progressively refined to resolve discrepancies while preserving interpretability.

Visualizing Relationships Between Overall Entities, Subgroups, and Individual Actors

Visualization emerges as a potent instrument for facilitating communication and analyzing hierarchical structures within intricate systems. Well-crafted visualizations transform abstract relationships into intuitive representations that unveil patterns and insights that might remain concealed in purely numerical or textual descriptions. Several visualization approaches demonstrate exceptional utility in hierarchical modeling. Nested treemaps[1] depict hierarchical structures employing nested rectangles, where rectangle size is typically proportional to a quantitative attribute such as the number of members, resource allocation, or activity level. Color coding can signify additional attributes, including objective type, growth rate, or risk level. Treemaps efficiently utilize screen space while effectively conveying hierarchical relationships and relative magnitudes.

Multi-level network diagrams depict actors as nodes and relationships as edges, with visual clustering indicating subgroup membership. Interactive implementations enable users to expand or collapse subgroups, facilitating seamless transitions between macro views that illustrate relationships between subgroups and micro views that reveal individual actors within them. Edge

---

[1] Treemaps are data visualization tools that display hierarchical data using nested rectangles. Each branch of the hierarchy is represented by a rectangle, which is then tiled with smaller rectangles representing sub-branches.

thickness, color, or style can signify relationship strength, type, or directionality.

Sunburst[2] diagrams provide radial visualizations that represent hierarchy through concentric rings, with the innermost circle representing the highest level of aggregation and outer rings representing progressively more granular levels. Angular segments correspond to distinct branches within the hierarchy. This approach is particularly effective for visualizing proportional relationships and nested categories.

Sankey[3] diagrams serve as effective flow diagrams, particularly useful for visualizing resource or information transfers between system components across hierarchical levels. The width of flow lines signifies the volume or intensity of the transfer, while color can represent the diverse types of resources or information being exchanged.

For systems characterized by intricate hierarchical structures, three-dimensional visualizations can augment representational dimensions. These visualizations may encompass cone trees, information cubes, or virtual reality implementations, enabling analysts to traverse hierarchical data spatially.

---

[2] Sunburst diagrams radial visualizations that display hierarchical data using concentric rings. Each ring represents a level in the hierarchy, with the innermost circle representing the root node and outer rings showing deeper hierarchical levels.

[3] Sankey are flow visualizations that display quantities in proportion to one another, with the width of the flows representing the quantity of the resource being transferred.

The most effective visualizations often incorporate interactive elements that enable dynamic filtering, semantic zooming, temporal animation, cross-sectional views, and comparative juxtaposition. Dynamic filtering selectively displays system components based on specified criteria. Semantic zooming reveals additional detail as users focus on particular system regions. Temporal animation demonstrates how hierarchical structures evolve over time. Cross-sectional views facilitate switching between different structural perspectives or attribute emphases. Comparative juxtaposition displays multiple hierarchical representations side-by-side for comparison.

When designing visualizations, several principles should guide development. Clarity should precede complexity, prioritizing clear communication of essential relationships over comprehensive inclusion of all system details. Appropriate abstraction aligns visualization granularity with analytical objectives. Consistent visual grammar ensures consistent visual encoding across representation levels. Perceptual accessibility designs consider human perceptual capabilities. Contextual preservation ensures that zoomed or filtered views maintain contextual reference to the broader system.

Through thoughtful visualization, hierarchical models become more accessible, enabling both analysts and stakeholders to develop an intuitive understanding of complex system structures that would remain impenetrable in purely formal representations.

Tracing Information, Resource, and Influence Flows

In addition to static structural representation, hierarchical models must capture the dynamic flows that animate intricate systems. These flows, whether of information, resources, or influence, expose how system components interact across hierarchical levels and how these interactions engender emergent system behaviors.

Information flows encompass the transmission of data, knowledge, directives, and feedback throughout the system. In numerous complex systems, information is the primary coordinator of decentralized activity. Mapping these flows necessitates identifying information types, transmission mechanisms, processing transformations, temporal characteristics, and accessibility constraints.

Various categories of information, such as operational directives, strategic guidance, status updates, and environmental intelligence, may traverse distinct pathways. Information circulates between actors through formal reporting, informal communication, broadcast announcements, and observed behaviors. Information traverses hierarchical levels and transforms into aggregation, filtering, amplification, and reframing. Timing patterns encompass frequency, latency, sequencing, and synchronization. Access restrictions determine which actors gain access to which information and the barriers that impede wider distribution.

Resource flows monitor the movement of tangible and intangible assets throughout the system. These may include financial capital, physical materials, human effort, technological capabilities, or reputational assets. Resource flow analysis scrutinizes allocation mechanisms, transformation processes, efficiency metrics, dependency relationships, and buffering capacities.

Resources are distributed across system components through centralized planning, market mechanisms, or mutually agreed-upon agreements. As resources traverse the system, they undergo transformations—raw materials evolve into finished products, and financial capital transforms into operational capabilities. Efficiency metrics elucidate the extent to which resources are utilized, thereby identifying bottlenecks, surpluses, and waste. Resource flows establish dependencies between system components. Systems effectively manage resource variability through inventories, reserves, and redundancies.

The Influence Flows Map illustrates the propagation of behavioral changes throughout a system. When an actor modifies its behavior, it often triggers adaptive responses from connected actors, resulting in cascades of influence that can reshape system dynamics. Influence analysis encompasses authority structures, persuasion networks, reinforcement patterns, threshold effects, and resistance mechanisms.

Formal and informal power relationships enable certain actors to direct the behaviors of others. Actors influence one another through non-coercive means such as demonstration, argumentation, or incentivization. Behaviors are reinforced or weakened through feedback loops. At specific thresholds, incremental influence accumulates to trigger qualitative behavioral shifts. System components maintain autonomous behavior despite attempts to exert external influence through various resistance mechanisms.

Analysts employ a combination of methodologies to effectively trace these flows, including process mapping, event analysis, network analysis, time-series analysis, and agent-based simulation.

Process mapping documents standard operating procedures and routine interactions that structure regular flows. Event analysis examines specific incidents to identify how flows operated in particular circumstances. Network analysis applies graph theory to identify pathways, bottlenecks, and central nodes in flow networks. Time-series analysis tracks temporal patterns to identify sequences, delays, and rhythms in system flows. Agent-based simulation models how flows emerge from individual actor behaviors and interactions.

By integrating flow analysis with hierarchical structural models, we establish a comprehensive comprehension of intricate systems. This comprehension encompasses not only their organizational structure but also their dynamic functioning through continuous interactions among components. This understanding facilitates predicting system responses to disturbances, the identification of intervention points for system modifications, and the recognition of early warning indicators for potential system transitions.

Case Study: Applying Hierarchical Modeling to System Transformation

To illustrate the practical application of hierarchical modeling principles, we present a case study involving a large-scale transformation initiative. This initiative encompasses a complex multi-agent system comprising numerous subgroups, each pursuing distinct yet interdependent objectives.

A substantial organization with operations spanning multiple regions initiated a comprehensive transformation program to modernize its core processes, external partnerships, and internal operations. This initiative engaged multiple functional areas, external collaborators, and newly established specialized teams operating across diverse organizational levels.

Our analysis commenced by identifying the key subgroups involved in the transformation endeavor. At the apex of this hierarchy stood a leadership group, responsible for guiding strategic direction and resource allocation. A central coordination team was subsequently established to facilitate the synchronization of transformation activities across the organization. Various functional implementation teams were tasked with adapting novel solutions to specific operational domains. A technical support group was dedicated to developing and maintaining the underlying systems. External partners were engaged to provide specialized capabilities. A network of change facilitators was employed to facilitate the adoption of the new systems at local levels. Finally, the end participants whose daily activities would be directly impacted by the newly implemented systems constituted the foundation of this hierarchical structure.

We meticulously documented each subgroup's key characteristics, including decision-making authority, resource accessibility, technical proficiency, institutional experience, and transformation-specific objectives. This comprehensive mapping unveiled substantial variation in priorities. While the leadership group prioritized long-term strategic outcomes and investment returns, implementation teams focused on ensuring operational continuity and minimizing disruption. At the same time, end participants emphasized practical utility and user-friendliness.

Hierarchical Model Construction

We have developed a four-tier hierarchical model to represent the transformation system. The top tier encompasses the overarching transformation program, its strategic objectives, and boundary conditions. The second tier represents functional areas and their specific transformation components. The third tier includes cross-functional working groups and specialized technical teams. The fourth tier identifies key individuals with substantial influence or specialized roles.

The model exhibits a hybrid structure that integrates traditional hierarchical relationships with matrix elements and emergent communities of practice. Visualization utilizing an interactive network diagram facilitates stakeholders' navigation between tiers, enabling them to assess formal and informal relationships impacting transformation outcomes.

Flow Analysis

Analyzing the flow of information through this hierarchical structure provided critical insights. Information flows revealed significant bottlenecks between technical teams and functional units, often resulting in the loss of technical specifications during translation and the misinterpretation of practical requirements. The analysis identified informal connectors—individuals without formal authority who nevertheless facilitated effective communication across organizational boundaries due to their unique positioning and relationship networks.

Resource flows uncovered an uneven distribution of transformation investments, with certain areas receiving disproportionate allocations relative to their strategic importance. Temporal analysis of resource deployment revealed problematic sequencing, with some teams receiving necessary tools only after achieving key implementation milestones.

Influence flows mapped how adoption behaviors spread throughout the organization, revealing that peer influence among end participants had a greater impact on acceptance than formal directives from leadership. The analysis identified key opinion shapers whose demonstrated usage patterns significantly influenced colleagues' adoption decisions.

Visualization and Communication

We devised a dynamic visualization that surpassed conventional representations to render this intricate analysis comprehensible to stakeholders. This interactive tool permitted viewers to transition between structural and functional views, emphasize information, resource, and influence flows through color-coded pathways, zoom from system-level overviews to individual team configurations, observe the temporal evolution of the transformation network across the program timeline, and filter the visualization based on specific components, processes, or outcome metrics. This visualization fulfilled multiple objectives. For leaders, it provided a comprehensive view of transformation progress and interdependence. For implementation teams, it underscores collaboration opportunities and potential conflicts. For the coordination team, it served as a diagnostic tool to identify emerging issues before they escalated into critical problems.

Key Insights and Outcomes

The hierarchical modeling approach unveiled several insights that would have remained concealed through conventional analysis. We identified cross-level misalignments between strategic objectives at the system level and implementation realities at the team level. While leaders emphasized comprehensive integration, implementation teams prioritized short-term operational continuity, resulting in divergent trajectories.

The analysis uncovered influential subgroups outside the formal structure, but significantly impacted transformation outcomes. These included communities of practice that spanned functional boundaries and informal advisory networks that influenced solution design.

Temporal analysis revealed how implementation approaches evolved as teams gained experience from early endeavors. These adaptations were largely imperceptible to leadership but represented valuable innovations that could be scaled across the organization.

The model identified areas where resource allocations deviated from stated priorities, creating implementation gaps that jeopardized program success.

Based on these insights, several interventions were implemented. Cross-functional coordination teams were established at pivotal interfaces. Formal knowledge-sharing mechanisms were established to capture and disseminate emerging best practices. Resource allocation was realigned to align with strategic priorities. Informal influencers were identified and empowered to serve as transformation ambassadors.

These interventions resulted in tangible improvements in implementation speed, solution adoption, and ultimately system outcomes from the transformation program.

Reflection on the Approach

This case study exemplifies the efficacy of hierarchical modeling in comprehending intricate multi-agent systems. Through systematic identification of subgroups, delineating their boundaries and objectives, constructing multi-level representations, visualization of relationships, and tracing of flows, we gained a comprehensive understanding of system dynamics that facilitated targeted interventions.

This approach surpasses conventional organizational analysis by acknowledging the coexistence of formal structures and emergent patterns, explicitly representing cross-level interactions, and capturing dynamic flows that animate the static structural framework. The resulting model provided a snapshot of system configuration and a dynamic representation of how information, resources, and influence traversed the system to generate observable outcomes.

The hierarchical modeling approach presents a potent framework for initial system conceptualization, the pivotal initial step preceding the effective application of more specialized analytical methods. By clearly comprehending system structure, component relationships, and dynamic flows, we establish the necessary foundation for all subsequent analysis.

CHAPTER 3

Data Acquisition and Preparation

The efficacy of any intricate systems analysis is intrinsically linked to the quality, comprehensiveness, and relevance of the underlying data. Data acquisition and preparation become pivotal foundations for subsequent analytical endeavors as we progress from conceptual frameworks to practical implementation. This chapter explores methodologies for collecting, processing, and transforming data, enabling robust multi-agent system analysis.

Complex systems composed of independent actors generate and respond to diverse data types, each offering unique insights into system functioning. A comprehensive analytical approach necessitates integrating these disparate data streams to establish a multidimensional comprehension.

Time series data captures the evolution of system variables over time, providing crucial insights into temporal patterns, trends, and rhythms. Several categories of time series data demonstrate exceptional value for the analysis of complex systems.

Quantitative Indicators of System Outcomes and Effectiveness

In financial markets, these indicators may include asset prices, trading volumes, and volatility measures. In healthcare systems, they encompass patient outcomes, resource utilization rates, and treatment efficacy statistics.

Measurements that Track Agent Actions Over Time

These indicators may include transaction frequencies, communication patterns, movement trajectories, or resource allocation decisions. The temporal evolution of these behaviors reveals adaptation patterns and response mechanisms.

Environmental variables, which originate outside system boundaries but influence system functioning, are labeled as such. These variables may include regulatory changes, technological innovations, demographic shifts, or macroeconomic indicators. Environmental time series provide crucial context for interpreting system dynamics.

Internal state measurements, also known as indicators of system components' internal conditions, are measurements taken to assess a system component's current state. In organizational contexts, these indicators may include employee satisfaction metrics, stress levels, or confidence indicators. Ecological systems could encompass energy reserves, health status, or reproductive capacity of constituent organisms.

Time-series data is characterized by its sequential nature and temporal dependence. Analysis must account for various temporal characteristics.

The interval between consecutive observations, known as the sampling frequency, represents the time interval between data points. The total duration covered by the data is referred to as the duration. Cyclic patterns occurring at regular intervals are characterized by seasonality. Directional movements over extended periods are termed trends, while abrupt changes or regime shifts signify discontinuities. Under stationarity, statistical properties remain constant over time.

The acquisition of high-quality time-series data presents several challenges. Maintaining consistent sampling methodologies over extended periods is challenging, especially when measurement systems evolve. Retrospective data often suffers from varying quality standards and methodological inconsistencies. Automated collection systems may experience technical failures, resulting in gaps requiring appropriate analysis handling.

Despite these challenges, time-series data offers invaluable insights into system evolution. It facilitates the identification of causal relationships, the prediction of future states, and the detection of critical transitions that might otherwise remain concealed in static snapshots.

Additional data types are listed below as important sources.

Network data captures the relationships and interactions between system components, revealing structural patterns that influence system dynamics. Various network types may coexist in intricate multi-agent systems, each representing distinct relationship dimensions:

- Communication networks delineate the information exchange pathways between agents. These networks record the communicators, the frequency of communication, the channels utilized, and the content characteristics conveyed. Communication networks frequently function as primary coordination mechanisms within decentralized systems.

- Transaction networks facilitate the exchange of resources, commodities, or services. These networks meticulously record the parties involved in transactions, the volume and monetary value of exchanges, and temporal patterns of transactions. Transaction networks unveil economic relationships and resource distribution mechanisms.

- Influence networks elucidate how agents influence one another's behaviors and decisions. These networks can be inferred from behavioral correlations, explicit references, or direct reporting of influence sources. They expose power structures and persuasion pathways that may exist independently of formal authority relationships.

- Physical proximity networks document the spatial co-location of agents. In numerous systems, physical proximity facilitates other forms of interaction and is a prerequisite for relationship formation. Contemporary data collection systems, such as mobile device tracking, Bluetooth proximity sensing, and video analytics, enable increasingly precise proximity mapping.

- Affiliation networks encompass shared memberships within groups, organizations, or categories. These networks frequently serve as the foundations for information sharing, trust development, and identity formation, subsequently influencing system dynamics.

Network data is typically represented as graphs, where nodes correspond to agents, and edges signify relationships. These relationships may possess various attributes, such as direction to indicate whether relationships are unidirectional or reciprocal, weight to denote the strength or intensity of relationships, type to categorize distinct relationship forms, temporality to specify when relationships are formed, persist, and dissolve, and multiplexity to describe the relationship types existing between the same agents.

The acquisition of network data presents distinct challenges. Comprehensive network mapping necessitates near-exhaustive sampling of the population, as the absence of certain nodes can substantially distort structural metrics. Self-reported relationship data frequently exhibits recall biases, social desirability effects, and definitional ambiguities. Behavioral or transactional relationship indicators offer more objective indicators but may overlook cognitive or affective dimensions of relationships.

Despite these challenges, network data provides an indispensable structural context for comprehending system dynamics. Network analysis elucidates how information, resources, and influence are disseminated through systems, identifies critical junctures and bottlenecks, and elucidates why seemingly congruent interventions may yield markedly divergent outcomes depending on their application within network structures.

Textual data encompasses written or transcribed communication between agents, formal documentation of system rules and procedures, narrative accounts of system events, and expressions of agent perceptions and intentions. This unstructured data source provides rich contextual information that is often absent from quantitative measurements.

Communication content encompasses messages exchanged between agents through various text-based channels, such as emails, instant messages, social media, formal reports, and others. These communications reveal coordination mechanisms, emerging concerns, information sharing practices, and evolving narratives contributing to system understanding.

Procedural documentation, on the other hand, captures formal codifications of rules, roles, processes, and expectations. This documentation includes policy manuals, standard operating procedures, legal frameworks, and regulatory guidelines establishing boundary conditions for agent behavior.

Narrative accounts describe system events, developments, and transitions from participant perspectives. They may include incident reports, after-action reviews, journalistic accounts, or historical narratives that provide interpretive context for observed behaviors.

Statements of goals, plans, strategies, and rationales convey intentions. These encompass strategic plans, mission statements, public announcements, or personal communications that elucidate how agents comprehend their objectives and justify their actions.

Textual data captures nuanced explanations and justifications that quantitative data alone cannot provide. Furthermore, textual expressions often reveal goals and motivations that drive observable behaviors.

Written documents demonstrate how agents interpret events and construct shared meanings. These are valuable records of often causal sequences and developmental arcs that quantitative snapshots overlook.

The acquisition and processing of textual data present distinct challenges. Text generation is unevenly distributed across agent populations, with more vocal or literate agents producing disproportionate volumes. Document access often entails navigating privacy concerns, confidentiality restrictions, and proprietary limitations. The sheer volume of text in many systems necessitates automated processing approaches that may compromise nuance for scalability.

Modern natural language processing techniques have significantly enhanced our ability to derive structured insights from unstructured text. Sentiment analysis quantifies emotional tone, topic modeling identifies thematic patterns, entity recognition extracts references to key system components, and semantic network analysis maps conceptual relationships. LLMs now enable increasingly sophisticated summarization, categorization, and interpretation of textual corpora at scales previously unmanageable.

By integrating textual analysis with quantitative approaches, we gain a comprehensive understanding of what transpires in complex systems and the reasons behind those occurrences. We combine observable behaviors with expressed intentions and interpretations that drive those behaviors.

Discrete exchanges or interactions between agents fall under the umbrella of transactional data, capturing the detailed fabric of system operations. These granular records document specific instances of resource exchange, service provision, information sharing, or other interaction types that collectively constitute system functioning.

Records of monetary exchanges, including purchases, sales, investments, loans, and payments. These transactions reveal resource flows, economic relationships, and value allocation patterns within transactional systems. They also document service provision events, including healthcare visits, customer support interactions, professional consultations, or educational sessions. These records capture how specialized capabilities are distributed throughout systems.

Digital platform activities encompass logs of user actions on digital systems, such as website visits, application usage, content consumption, and feature engagement. These digital footprints unveil patterns of information access, tool utilization, and virtual environment navigation.

Physical movements are records of agent relocations through transportation system usage, access control systems, or location tracking technologies. Movement data discloses spatial patterns, co-location possibilities, and physical resource allocation.

Transactional data typically encompasses several key elements: participating agents (identifiers for transaction initiators, recipients, and facilitators), temporal information (including the time of transaction occurrence, its duration, and its sequencing), content description (specifically detailing what was exchanged or what service was provided), volumetric measurement (quantities, values, or intensities associated with the transaction), and contextual attributes (such as the location, channel, method, or circumstances of the transaction).

Digital systems that automatically generate transaction records as byproducts of their normal operation have revolutionized the acquisition of transactional data. Point-of-sale systems, electronic medical records, online platforms, communication systems, and Internet of Things devices continuously generate unprecedented volumes of transactional data. This automated collection eliminates many traditional data-gathering limitations but introduces new challenges such as volume management, privacy protection, and meaningful pattern extraction from overwhelming detail.

Transactional data provides exceptional granularity for system analysis, enabling the reconstruction of precise interaction sequences, the identification of micro-patterns invisible in aggregated data, and the discovery of anomalous events that may indicate emerging system changes. Transactional data connects abstract system models to concrete operational realities when properly integrated into analytical frameworks, bridging theoretical understanding with practical application.

Source Selection Strategies and Data Analysis Techniques

When analyzing intricate systems, strategically selecting data sources becomes paramount. Instead of attempting to collect all conceivable data—an approach that quickly becomes impractical—analysts must prioritize sources based on specific analytical objectives, available resources, and practical limitations.

The selection process should commence with a clear understanding of analytical objectives. Different inquiries naturally necessitate distinct types of data. For causal comprehension, longitudinal time-series data with high temporal resolution and control variables should be prioritized. When mapping structural relationships, comprehensive network data capturing pertinent relationship dimensions becomes most valuable. Behavioral prediction relies on detailed transactional records with consistent feature recording, while meaning interpretation benefits from extensive textual data representing diverse system viewpoints.

By aligning data acquisition with specific analytical objectives, researchers can effectively avoid data scarcity (insufficient information to address critical inquiries) and data overload (excessive information obscuring fundamental patterns).

Complex systems rarely reveal their true nature through a single data type.

Integrating multiple complementary sources provides triangulation that enhances validity and uncovers multidimensional insights. Several effective triangulation strategies exist:

- **Behavioral-cognitive pairing** combines objective behavioral records (what agents perform) with subjective cognitive data (how agents perceive their actions). This pairing uncovers disconnects between actions and interpretations that frequently drive system evolution. Macro-micro bridging integrates system-level aggregate measures with individual-level detailed records, connecting emergent patterns to constituent behaviors and elucidating how micro-dynamics generate macro-outcomes.

- **Quantitative-qualitative integration** seamlessly integrates numerical measurements with narrative explanations, offering both precise quantitative data and a comprehensive contextual understanding that neither approach alone can provide. Temporal-structural coordination harmonizes longitudinal time-series with structural network data, elucidating how relationships influence behavioral evolution and how behaviors, in turn, reshape relationship structures.

Effective triangulation necessitates meticulous consideration of how diverse data sources can synergistically complement each other's strengths and mitigate their respective limitations.

Practical Accessibility Considerations

Practical constraints significantly influence the selection of data sources. Accessibility considerations encompass legal access, technical accessibility, economic feasibility, and temporal availability.

Legal access entails navigating regulatory, privacy, proprietary, or security restrictions restricting data accessibility. Numerous valuable data sources in healthcare, finance, and criminal justice domains encounter substantial legal access constraints. Technical accessibility concerns whether data exists in formats that can be practically extracted, transformed, and integrated into analytical systems. Legacy systems, proprietary formats, and non-digital records frequently present technical barriers.

Economic feasibility refers to whether acquisition costs align with available resources. Commercial data sources often entail significant licensing fees, while primary data collection entails substantial operational costs. Temporal availability considers whether historical data exists for retrospective analysis and whether ongoing data collection is feasible for prospective monitoring. Many systems lack consistent historical records, thereby limiting longitudinal analysis.

A realistic accessibility assessment facilitates the avoidance of investing in data acquisition pathways that ultimately fail to deliver the required information, enabling efforts to be directed toward more feasible alternatives.

---

*Not all available data sources meet the quality standards
necessary for reliable analysis.*

Key quality dimensions include completeness, accuracy, consistency, representativeness, and granularity:

- **Completeness** ensures that the data encompasses all pertinent system components, time periods, and variables. Fragmentary data with substantial gaps may introduce erroneous patterns.

- **Accuracy** assesses whether recorded values reliably reflect actual conditions. Measurement error, recording errors, and intentional misrepresentation all compromise accuracy.

- **Consistency** examines whether collection methods, definitions, and recording practices remain consistent across the dataset. Methodological inconsistencies create artificial patterns that reflect measurement changes rather than system dynamics.

- **Representativeness** concerns whether available data accurately reflects the entire system rather than a biased subset. Selection biases in data collection can lead to a significantly distorted understanding.

- **Granularity** addresses whether the data provides sufficient detail to address specific analytical questions. Overly aggregated data may conceal important variations and patterns. Formal quality evaluation frameworks help systematize these assessments, enabling informed decisions about which sources warrant investment and which should be approached with caution or excluded entirely.

Ethical Dimensions of Data Selection

In addition to practical considerations, ethical dimensions should guide the selection of data sources. Key ethical considerations include obtaining informed consent, safeguarding privacy, addressing equity implications, and mitigating dual-use concerns:

- **Informed consent** ensures that data subjects have provided comprehensive consent for their data to be utilized for analytical purposes, particularly when analysis extends beyond the original collection objectives. Privacy protection safeguards sensitive personal information throughout the data lifecycle, from acquisition to analysis and storage.

- **Equity implications** assess whether data collection practices systematically exclude or distort specific populations, potentially resulting in biased interpretations and discriminatory applications. Dual-use concerns evaluate whether analyses may facilitate harmful applications beyond their intended purposes, particularly in security, surveillance, or manipulation contexts.

- **Ethical data selection** upholds human dignity, fosters trust with stakeholders, and prevents analytical outcomes that inadvertently perpetuate existing inequalities or facilitate harmful applications.

Raw data rarely presents itself in forms immediately suitable for intricate systems analysis.

Preprocessing transforms raw data into analyzable formats, addresses quality concerns, and establishes the groundwork for feature engineering and modeling. Three critical preprocessing challenges warrant specific attention.

Handling Missing Values

Missing data poses a substantial challenge in complex systems analysis. It originates from diverse sources, such as collection failures, non-response, selective reporting, and inherent gaps in observability. Several approaches are employed to effectively address this challenge.

Firstly, detection and quantification are paramount. Before implementing solutions, analysts must conduct a comprehensive assessment of missingness patterns. Random missingness, characterized by the occurrence of missing values by chance, necessitates a distinct approach compared to systematic missingness, which involves the specific types of values being more prone to missing. Visualization tools, such as missingness maps, facilitate the identification of patterns, while quantitative metrics, including missingness rates by variable and observation, provide precise measurements.

Complete-case analysis involves excluding observations with missing values from the analysis. While straightforward, this approach risks introducing selection bias if there is a correlation between missingness and substantive variables. In network analysis, node removal poses particular challenges as it affects structural measures for all connected nodes.

Imputation methods estimate missing values based on available information. Simple imputation utilizes statistical measures like mean, median, or mode to fill gaps. More sophisticated approaches include k-nearest neighbor[4] imputation (utilizing similar observations' values), regression imputation (predicting missing values from other variables), and multiple imputations (generating multiple plausible values to represent uncertainty).

Model-based approaches explicitly incorporate missingness into analytical models. Maximum likelihood estimation with missing data employs all available information while accounting for

---

[4] K-Nearest Neighbors is a simple, intuitive machine learning algorithm used for both classification and regression tasks. It works on the fundamental principle that similar data points tend to exist close to each other.

missingness patterns. Bayesian approaches incorporate prior knowledge about probable values and their distributions.

Redesigning collection processes for future data may be necessary when missingness presents severe analytical limitations. This may involve incorporating redundant measurement pathways, implementing quality control checks, or creating incentives for complete reporting.

The appropriate missing data strategy depends on the specific missingness patterns, analytical objectives, and available resources. While sophisticated approaches yield more reliable results, they require greater computational resources and statistical expertise.

Outliers in Complex Systems Data

Outlier observations that significantly deviate from typical patterns present both challenges and opportunities for intricate systems analysis. They may signify measurement inaccuracies requiring rectification, exceptional yet valid system states offering valuable insights, or early indicators of system transitions warranting specialized attention.

Detection methodologies identify potential outliers through diverse approaches. Statistical methods identify observations surpassing specified thresholds (e.g., three standard deviations from the mean) or based on distribution characteristics (e.g., Tukey's fences[5] utilizing interquartile ranges). Distance-based methods like Local Outlier Factor quantify the isolation of points from neighboring observations. Density-based algorithms like DBSCAN[6] identify points in low-density regions of the data space. Model-based techniques like isolation forests explicitly construct decision rules to separate outlying observations.

Once potential outliers are identified, systematic investigation helps determine their nature. This encompasses data provenance verification (ensuring collection and processing accuracy), contextual assessment (evaluating whether unusual environmental conditions account for the deviation), and domain expert consultation (utilizing specialized knowledge about plausible system states).

Management strategies differ based on investigation outcomes. Confirmed measurement errors necessitate correction or exclusion from analysis. Genuine outliers representing exceptional, yet valid system states should generally be retained but may require robust analytical methods that minimize their disproportionate influence on results. Early warning signals warrant specialized analytical attention, potentially triggering more frequent monitoring or contingency planning.

---

[5] Tukey's fences are a method for identifying outliers in statistical data based on quartiles.

[6] DBSCAN is a popular density-based clustering algorithm that groups together points that are closely packed while marking points in low-density regions as outliers.

Thoughtful outlier management balances statistical rigor and domain understanding, avoiding the uncritical inclusion of erroneous values and the inappropriate exclusion of unusual yet informative observations.

Comprehensive validation procedures ensure the overall integrity of the data. They systematically verify that the data meets quality standards before it is entered into analytical pipelines, in addition to addressing specific missing value and outlier challenges.

Internal consistency checks validate logical relationships between variables within datasets. For instance, they ensure that timestamps follow proper sequences, categorical variables contain only allowed values, and mathematical relationships between derived variables are maintained. Cross-source verification compares data elements that should match across multiple sources. Discrepancies may indicate collection or integration errors that require resolution before analysis proceeds.

Temporal stability assessment examines whether variable distributions remain consistent over periods when stability is expected. Sudden distribution changes often signal collection methodology changes rather than genuine system shifts. Where available, reference data comparison validates key metrics against authoritative external references. Significant unexplained deviations from established benchmarks warrant investigation.

Expert review engages domain specialists to assess whether data patterns align with professional knowledge and experience.

Experts often identify implausible values or relationships that automated validation might miss. Validation procedures should be formalized into reproducible routines that can be applied consistently across datasets and time periods.

> *Documentation of validation processes and results enhances analytical transparency and builds stakeholder confidence in subsequent findings.*

Feature Engineering Approaches

Raw data typically lacks variables in optimal formats for intricate systems analysis. Feature engineering transforms raw data elements into pertinent representations that more accurately capture system attributes and augment analytical capabilities. This transformation process necessitates both domain expertise and technical proficiency.

Extracting Temporal Features

Time-series data can be enhanced by incorporating features that capture dynamic patterns beyond mere sequential values. Moving statistics calculate rolling means, medians, standard deviations, minimums, and maximums over predetermined time intervals. These features effectively mitigate noise while preserving trend information and providing local context for point measurements.

Rate-of-change indicators compute first and second derivatives (representing velocity and acceleration) to discern the rate of change of variables and whether the change is accelerating or decelerating. These dynamics often exhibit superior predictive capabilities compared to absolute values. Volatility measures calculate variance, coefficient of variation, or other dispersion metrics over time windows to quantify stability or turbulence. Numerous intricate systems exhibit distinctive volatility patterns prior to critical transitions.

Periodicity features employ Fourier transforms[7] or wavelet analysis to discern cyclic patterns at varying time scales. These techniques unveil concealed rhythms that may influence system behavior but remain imperceptible in raw time-series data. Lag features generate variables representing preceding values at predetermined time intervals. These facilitate models in capturing temporal dependencies and autocorrelation structures.

Temporal relationship features compute lead/lag correlations between distinct variables to identify potential causal relationships or mutual influences with time delays. Event duration measurements convert timestamp data into duration measurements for processes, states, or intervals between recurrent events. Duration frequently provides more pertinent information than raw timestamps.

---

[7] Fourier transforms are mathematical techniques that decompose functions into their constituent frequencies.

By transforming raw temporal data into these engineered features, analysts facilitate the detection of patterns and relationships that would remain imperceptible in unprocessed time series.

Network Feature Engineering

Network data can be transformed into features that characterize positions, relationships, and structures:

- **Centrality measures** calculate metrics such as degree centrality (number of connections), betweenness centrality (frequency of positioning on shortest paths), closeness centrality (inverse average distance to all other nodes), or eigenvector centrality (connection to other central nodes). These metrics identify influential positions within networks.

- **Clustering coefficients** compute the proportion of potential connections among a node's neighbors that actually exist. This measure distinguishes tightly interconnected communities from loosely connected structures. Structural equivalence metrics calculate similarity in connection patterns between nodes, identifying actors who occupy similar structural positions irrespective of direct connection.

- Path-**based features** quantify characteristics such as average path length, diameter (maximum shortest path), and reachability between specific nodes. These features elucidate network navigability and the potential for information flow. Subgraph frequencies quantify the occurrences of specific network motifs or patterns that may serve as fundamental building blocks of the overall structure.

- **Dynamic network features**, applicable to time-varying networks, extract metrics such as link formation rates, community stability, and structural persistence, which capture evolutionary dynamics. These network features transform abstract connection patterns into quantitative indicators that can be integrated into predictive models, comparative analyses, or monitoring systems.

- **Textual data** necessitates transformation into structured features that encapsulate pertinent semantic content. Term frequency metrics quantify word or phrase occurrences, frequently weighted by inverse document frequency (TF-IDF) to prioritize distinctive rather than prevalent terms. These fundamental features capture topical content.

- **Word embeddings** convert words into numerical vectors that preserve semantic relationships, employing approaches such as Word2Vec,[8] GloVe, or contextual

---

[8] A group of neural network models used to produce word embeddings, which represent words as dense vectors in a continuous vector space where semantically similar words are mapped to nearby points.

embeddings derived from transformer models. These facilitate mathematical computations on textual meaning. Sentiment indicators compute scores representing emotional tone, opinion polarity, or affective content. These features capture subjective dimensions that are frequently critical for comprehending social systems.

- **Entity extraction** features identify and categorize mentions of specific individuals, organizations, locations, dates, or other entities referenced in text. These features facilitate the tracking of key system components across narratives. Topic proportions employ topic modeling techniques, such as Latent Dirichlet Allocation, to estimate the distribution of themes present in documents. These features capture thematic composition at various granularities.

- **Discourse markers** identify linguistic elements that indicate relationships between ideas, such as causal connections, contrasts, or temporal sequences. These features assist in mapping reasoning patterns and narrative structures. Network-based text features transform textual co-occurrence or reference patterns into network representations, enabling the application of network metrics to semantic relationships.

> *Analysts can quantitatively incorporate rich semantic content into complex systems analysis by converting unstructured text into these structured features.*

Transactional data benefits from aggregation and pattern extraction to reveal behavioral signatures. Frequency features calculate transaction counts within time windows or across categories. Simple frequency often serves as a powerful indicator of engagement or activity levels.

Value distribution metrics compute statistical measures of transaction value distributions, including means, percentiles, variances, and extreme values. These capture volume patterns beyond simple counting. Temporal pattern features extract timing characteristics such as typical intervals between transactions, time-of-day patterns, day-of-week effects, or seasonality profiles. These reveal rhythmic behavioral signatures.

Sequence indicators identify recurring transaction sequences or patterns using techniques such as sequential pattern mining or Markov models.[9] These capture procedural regularities in behavior. Diversity metrics calculate measures of variety in transaction types, partners, or locations. Diversity often indicates distinct strategic approaches or roles within systems.

---

[9] Markov models are stochastic models used to model randomly changing systems where future states depend only on the current state and not on the sequence of events that preceded it.

Anomaly scores compute measures of deviation from typical transaction patterns for specific actors or time periods. These indicate potential regime changes or unusual activities warranting investigation. These engineered features transform granular transaction records into behavioral fingerprints that characterize how agents operate within complex systems.

Normalization and Standardization Methods

Features often exist on different scales with varying distributions, complicating comparative analysis and potentially biasing algorithms sensitive to scale differences. Normalization and standardization transform variables to comparable scales while preserving relative relationships.

Linear Scaling Approaches

These approaches transform variables to specified ranges while preserving proportional relationships. Min-max normalization rescales values to a fixed range (typically 0-1) using a formula that preserves relative positions but compresses all values into the target range, potentially minimizing the impact of outliers.

Decimal scaling shifts decimal points to create values between -1 and 1 by dividing by powers of 10, where the power is selected to achieve the desired range. This straightforward approach maintains interpretability for domain experts. Linear scaling approaches are intuitive and preserve relative distances between observations. Still, they can be susceptible to outliers that may compress most observations into a narrow segment of the target range.

Statistical Standardization Techniques

These techniques transform variables based on their distribution properties. Z-score[10] standardization rescales values to represent standard deviations from the mean, creating variables with a mean of 0 and a standard deviation of 1, enabling direct comparability. Z-scores are particularly useful for features that approximate normal distributions.

Robust scaling utilizes the median and interquartile range instead of the mean and standard deviation. This approach demonstrates reduced sensitivity to outliers compared to z-score standardization, making it valuable for skewed distributions or data with extreme values. Log transformation applies logarithmic scaling to compress wide ranges and address right-skewed distributions. Log transformations are particularly beneficial for variables spanning multiple orders of magnitude.

---

[10] Z-score (also called a standard score) measures how many standard deviations a data point is from the mean of its distribution.

Statistical standardization approaches acknowledge distribution characteristics but may present greater challenges for domain experts in terms of intuitive interpretation.

When linear approaches prove insufficient to address intricate distribution challenges, non-linear transformations offer viable alternatives. Quantile transformation assigns values to their percentile ranks within the distribution, subsequently transforming them to conform to a predetermined distribution (typically normal). This approach effectively manages arbitrary distributions, albeit potentially altering relative distances between observations.

Power transformations apply exponents to reshape distributions. Box-Cox transformations automatically select the optimal exponent parameter to maximize normality. These transformations effectively address skewness, but they necessitate strictly positive values. Hyperbolic transformations employ functions such as the hyperbolic tangent to compress extreme values while preserving central behavior. These approaches effectively handle outliers without completely excluding them from the analysis.

Non-linear transformations can significantly enhance algorithm performance for problematic distributions, albeit potentially introducing features that pose challenges in interpreting within their domain context.

Domain-Specific Normalization

In addition to general mathematical transformations, domain expertise frequently recommends specific normalization techniques that are particularly well-suited to the system being analyzed. Ratio construction establishes dimensionless ratios between associated variables, such as efficiency ratios (output divided by input), utilization rates (used divided by available), or density measures (events divided by area). These naturally normalized metrics frequently exhibit greater significance than their constituent variables.

Creating composite indices involves synthesizing standardized measures derived from multiple variables, guided by domain expertise. These indices may encompass weighted combinations of indicators chosen to represent theoretical constructs. Reference normalization scales values relative to predefined reference points imbued with domain significance, such as regulatory thresholds, historical milestones, or theoretical optimums.

Functional transformations apply transformations predicated on established functional relationships within the domain, notably logarithmic scaling for variables exhibiting exponential growth patterns. By integrating system knowledge into the transformation process, domain-specific normalization augments analytical efficacy and enhances the interpretability of results.

Complex systems analysis frequently necessitates integrating data from multiple sources collected at varying times, frequencies, and temporal granularities. Temporal alignment ensures that these disparate sources can be effectively combined for coherent analysis.

Distinct data sources often record observations at disparate temporal resolutions—some may capture transactions at the millisecond level, while others may record daily or monthly aggregates.

Aggregation combines higher-frequency observations into lower-frequency units through summation, averaging, or other aggregation functions. This approach compromises temporal detail but facilitates integration with lower-resolution sources. Interpolation estimates values at intermediate time points between existing observations using linear, spline, or model-based approaches. This generates artificial precision and should be applied judiciously when actual processes entail discontinuous changes.

Multi-resolution modeling constructs analytical frameworks that explicitly incorporate data at varying temporal resolutions without necessitating conversion to a single time scale. These approaches preserve information at its original granularities while facilitating integrated analysis. The optimal resolution harmonization approach is contingent upon the nature of the underlying processes and the analytical objectives. Critical events or state transitions may transpire between observations in lower-frequency data, potentially leading to misinterpretation risks that must be meticulously managed.

Even when data is recorded at compatible resolutions, timing discrepancies may arise due to disparate collection systems, time zones, or reference frames. Temporal registration aligns these temporal disparities through reference time standardization and other methodologies to guarantee consistent temporal frameworks across datasets.

CHAPTER 4

Behavioral Fingerprinting Using Machine Learning

Having established a robust data foundation in the preceding chapter, we now turn to one of the most potent analytical approaches for comprehending intricate multi-agent systems: behavioral fingerprinting. This methodology utilizes machine learning techniques to discern and characterize distinctive patterns in how agents operate, thereby generating "fingerprints" that uniquely identify subgroups and elucidate their underlying characteristics.

Behavioral fingerprinting serves multiple pivotal functions. It facilitates the identification of inherent groupings within seemingly homogeneous populations, thereby unveiling concealed structure within intricate systems. It provides diagnostic indicators distinguishing between various operational modes, enabling rapid recognition of state transitions. It establishes benchmarks for customary behavior, supporting anomaly detection that can identify emerging threats or opportunities. Perhaps most significantly, it constructs interpretable representations of intricate behavioral patterns, rendering sophisticated systems more comprehensible to human analysts.

This chapter delves into the machine learning techniques that facilitate effective behavioral fingerprinting. We explore unsupervised learning approaches that identify natural groupings, time-series methods that capture temporal patterns, and anomaly detection algorithms that pinpoint unusual behaviors. We demonstrate how these technical approaches synergize with domain knowledge to construct behavioral fingerprints that yield actionable insights for system comprehension and management.

The initial challenge in behavioral fingerprinting is often identifying natural groupings within intricate systems. While some subgroups may be formally defined through organizational structures or explicit categories, many emerge organically through comparable behavioral patterns without official designation. Unsupervised learning techniques prove invaluable for discovering these natural groupings without necessitating predefined classification schemes.

K-means[11] clustering represents one of the most widely applied approaches for partitioning multivariate data into distinct groups. The algorithm assigns observations to k clusters by minimizing within-cluster variance while maximizing between-cluster separation. In the context of behavioral fingerprinting, k-means groups agents based on similarity in their behavioral features.

The process comprises several stages: feature selection, initialization, assignment, update, and iteration. Feature selection identifies behavioral variables distinguishing distinct agent types, such as activity frequencies, interaction patterns, resource usage characteristics, or temporal signatures. Initialization establishes cluster centers, either randomly or employing heuristic methods that enhance convergence. Assignment assigns each agent to the nearest cluster center based on distance in feature space. Update recalculates cluster centers as the mean of all agents assigned to each cluster. Iteration repeats the assignment and update steps until cluster memberships stabilize or a predetermined maximum iteration count is reached.

The resulting clusters represent groups of agents with similar behavioral characteristics, potentially revealing natural subgroups within the system. For example, in financial markets, k-means clustering might identify trader groups with distinct patterns of

---

[11] K-means is a popular unsupervised machine learning algorithm used for clustering data points into groups based on similarity.

transaction timing, risk preferences, and asset selection, revealing market segments not visible in formal classifications.

K-means offers several advantages for behavioral fingerprinting. Its computational efficiency enables application to large-scale systems with numerous agents.

The algorithm yields intuitively interpretable results, with cluster centers representing "typical" behavioral profiles for each group. Its iterative nature facilitates interactive refinement based on domain expertise.

However, limitations necessitate careful consideration. K-means assumes spherical clusters of comparable size, potentially overlooking intricate grouping structures. It necessitates pre-specifying the number of clusters (k), although techniques such as the elbow method, silhouette analysis, or gap statistics can assist in determining suitable values. The algorithm's sensitivity to initialization necessitates multiple runs with distinct starting points to attain stable solutions.

While k-means creates flat partitions, hierarchical clustering constructs nested groupings that reveal relationships between clusters at multiple levels of granularity. This approach aligns particularly well with complex systems that naturally exhibit hierarchical organization, where subgroups exist within larger groups, which themselves form components of even broader categories.

Hierarchical clustering encompasses two primary forms: agglomerative (bottom-up) and divisive (top-down). Agglomerative clustering commences with each agent as its own cluster and progressively merges analogous clusters until a singular cluster encompasses all agents. Divisive clustering, on the other hand, adopts an inverse approach, commencing with all agents in a single cluster and recursively dividing clusters until each agent establishes its own cluster.

Both approaches yield hierarchical structures depicted as dendrograms—tree diagrams that elucidate the sequence of merges or divisions. These visualizations elucidate multi-level relationships among behavioral groups, enabling analysts to comprehend the interconnections between subgroups and determine suitable levels of granularity for specific analytical endeavors.

Several distance metrics and linkage methods influence how hierarchical clustering defines similarity between agents and clusters. Distance metrics include Euclidean distance, Manhattan distance, cosine similarity, and correlation distance. Linkage methods include single linkage, complete linkage, average linkage, and Ward's method. The choice of metrics and linkage methods should reflect domain-specific understanding of what constitutes meaningful similarity between behavioral patterns.

Hierarchical clustering presents several advantages for behavioral fingerprinting. It unveils multilevel structures without the need for prior specification of cluster numbers. It accommodates diverse similarity measures, allowing for adaptation to domain-specific notions of behavioral similarity. The resulting dendrograms provide intuitive visualizations of relationship structures.

However, hierarchical methods generally incur higher computational requirements than k-means, restricting their application to extremely large agent populations without sampling. Additionally, they lack a natural mechanism for reassigning agents after initial clustering, potentially resulting in suboptimal outcomes for intricate datasets. These limitations can be mitigated through hybrid approaches that combine hierarchical methods with subsequent optimization steps.

Density-based methods take a fundamentally different approach to clustering, defining groups based on regions of high data density separated by regions of lower density. DBSCAN (Density-Based Spatial Clustering of Applications with Noise) represents the most widely applied algorithm in this category, offering particular advantages for behavioral fingerprinting in complex systems.

DBSCAN operates using a process that defines parameters, identifies neighbors, forms clusters, and classifies points. It automatically determines the number of clusters based on data density patterns. It offers significant advantages for behavioral fingerprinting, where the appropriate number of behavioral types may not be known in advance.

DBSCAN offers several advantages that are particularly pertinent to complex systems analysis. Unlike k-means, which presumes spherical clusters, DBSCAN can discern clusters of arbitrary shapes, effectively capturing intricate behavioral groupings that may exhibit non-linear patterns in feature space. The algorithm explicitly identifies outliers as noise points, distinguishing between established behavioral patterns and anomalous behaviors that deviate from any recognized group. The parameters possess intuitive interpretations of behavioral similarity thresholds and minimum group sizes, facilitating domain-expert specification. Moreover, DBSCAN's automatic determination of cluster numbers enables the identification of emerging behavioral groups without prior assumptions regarding the number of distinct patterns.

Variations and extensions of DBSCAN further enhance its utility for behavioral fingerprinting. OPTICS addresses DBSCAN's sensitivity to density parameter selection by calculating a reachability plot that simultaneously identifies clusters across multiple density levels. HDBSCAN combines density-based clustering with hierarchical approaches, producing a hierarchy of density-based clusters that reveals multi-level behavioral patterns while handling varying density regions. ST-DBSCAN extends the algorithm to explicitly incorporate both spatial and temporal dimensions, which is particularly valuable for analyzing behaviors that evolve over time and space.

Through density-based clustering, analysts can identify natural behavioral groupings even when they form complex shapes in feature space, distinguish established patterns from anomalous behaviors, and discover patterns without preconceptions about the number of distinct behavioral types that exist.

Complex systems frequently exhibit distinctive temporal patterns, including rhythms, cycles, trends, and state transitions that characterize their dynamic behavior. Time-series analysis methodologies extract these patterns to construct temporal behavioral fingerprints that elucidate the evolution of agents and systems over time.

Autoregressive Integrated Moving Average (ARIMA) models constitute a foundational approach to time-series analysis, effectively capturing linear temporal dependencies in behavioral data. ARIMA models have three distinct components: autoregressive, integrated, and moving average. The autoregressive component elucidates the dependence of current values on preceding values. The integrated component addresses non-stationarity through differencing. The moving average component elucidates the dependence of current values on preceding forecast errors.

The ARIMA modeling process typically involves the following steps:

1. **Stationarity testing**: Ensures that the time series is stationary.
2. **Differencing**: Transforms the time series to make it stationary.

3. **Model identification**: Determines the appropriate order of the ARIMA model (p, d, q).

4. **Parameter estimation**: Estimates the parameters of the identified model.

5. **Diagnostic checking**: Checks the residuals of the model for any signs of non-stationarity or other issues.

6. **Forecasting**: Generates forecasts based on the estimated model parameters.

ARIMA models provide concise representations of temporal behavioral patterns, capturing linear dependencies that characterize many real-world processes. Their parameters offer interpretable insights into system memory and temporal horizon.

ARIMA models can discern between agents with distinct temporal characteristics for behavioral fingerprinting. For instance, in financial markets, certain traders may exhibit ARIMA(1,0,0) patterns indicating short-term momentum following, while others may exhibit ARIMA(0,1,1) patterns suggesting responses to unexpected market movements.

Extensions of basic ARIMA models augment their utility for behavioral fingerprinting. SARIMA incorporates seasonal patterns, capturing behaviors that follow daily, weekly, monthly, or other cyclic patterns. ARIMAX incorporates external factors that influence the time series, enabling models to account for known environmental conditions affecting behavior. Vector ARIMA models simultaneously analyze multiple interrelated time series, capturing dynamic interactions between different behavioral indicators.

While ARIMA models excel at capturing linear temporal dependencies, they encounter limitations in modeling highly non-linear dynamics prevalent in complex systems. Consequently, we explore more flexible approaches, such as LSTM networks.

Long Short-Term Memory (LSTM) networks constitute a specialized class of recurrent neural networks specifically designed to capture intricate temporal dependencies in sequential data. Unlike ARIMA models, LSTMs can model highly non-linear relationships and retain information across diverse time scales, making them highly valuable for complex behavioral fingerprinting.

The LSTM architecture comprises memory cells that store information over time, governed by gates controlling information flow: input gate, forget gate, and output gate. This architecture enables LSTMs to discern when to retain and discard information—a pivotal capability for identifying intricate behavioral patterns across varying time horizons.

LSTMs provide several advantages for behavioral fingerprinting. They can identify sequential patterns in behavior, specifically action sequences that characterize distinct agent types. They can simultaneously capture short-term tactical patterns and long-term strategic behaviors. LSTMs can model complex non-linear dependencies between past and present behaviors. Unlike statistical models necessitating manual feature engineering, LSTMs can learn relevant temporal features directly from raw data.

Implementing Long Short-Term Memory (LSTM) models for behavioral fingerprinting encompasses a comprehensive workflow, including sequence preparation, network architecture design, training configuration, training and validation, and feature extraction. LSTM models have exhibited exceptional efficacy in identifying behavioral patterns across diverse domains. In the context of cybersecurity, they effectively detect user authentication patterns that distinguish authentic users from unauthorized individuals. In healthcare, they recognize temporal signatures in patient data that serve as predictive indicators of adverse events. Furthermore, in transportation systems, they discern behavioral patterns of vehicles or pedestrians to anticipate their intended movements.

Despite their power, LSTMs present challenges including computational intensity, large data requirements, and reduced interpretability compared to statistical models. These limitations can be partially addressed through careful architecture design, transfer learning approaches, and techniques for extracting interpretable features from trained networks.

Hidden Markov Models[12] (HMMs) provide a probabilistic framework for modeling systems that transition between unobservable (hidden) states that generate observable outputs. This framework aligns naturally with many complex systems where underlying agent states (intentions, strategies, conditions) cannot be directly observed but produce observable behaviors.

HMMs consist of several components: hidden states, observations, transition probabilities, emission probabilities, and initial state distribution. HMMs address three fundamental questions for behavioral fingerprinting: evaluation, decoding, and learning. Evaluation assesses how well a particular behavioral model fits observed data. Decoding reveals the likely internal states that agents transitioned through. Learning enables the construction of behavioral models from empirical data.

Hidden Markov Models (HMMs) offer particularly valuable insights for behavioral fingerprinting by revealing concealed states, capturing state transitions, providing probabilistic interpretations, and enabling anomaly detection. Implementing HMMs for behavioral fingerprinting entails the following steps: state space definition, feature selection, parameter estimation, model validation, and state sequence decoding.

---

[12] Hidden Markov Models (HMMs) are statistical models used to represent systems that transition between hidden states, with only observable outputs or emissions associated with each state. They're particularly useful for modeling sequential data where the underlying state is not directly observable.

Hidden Markov Models (HMMs) have demonstrated efficacy across a wide range of application domains. In financial markets, they identify distinct regimes such as "trend-following," "mean-reversion," or "volatility breakout" that traders transition between. In healthcare, they recognize patient state transitions between "stable," "deteriorating," and "recovering" conditions. In cybersecurity, they detect transitions between "reconnaissance," "exploitation," and "data exfiltration" phases in attack sequences.

Extensions to fundamental HMMs augment their utility for complex behavioral modeling. Hierarchical HMMs model nested state structures, with higher-level states encompassing sequences of lower-level states. Input-Output HMMs incorporate external factors that influence state transitions, capturing how environmental conditions impact behavioral switching. Factorial HMMs model multiple independent state processes simultaneously, representing agents with multiple concurrent behavioral dimensions.

By identifying latent states and transition patterns, HMMs provide interpretable behavioral fingerprints that encapsulate the underlying dynamics of how agents operate and evolve over time.

Advanced Anomaly Detection and Application

While characterizing typical behavioral patterns provides valuable system comprehension, identifying anomalous behaviors often yields particularly crucial insights. Anomalies may represent emerging threats, innovative approaches, system malfunctions, or early indicators of broader transformations. Anomaly detection algorithms identify behaviors that deviate significantly from established patterns, serving as an indispensable component of comprehensive behavioral fingerprinting.

Isolation Forest is an efficient algorithm specifically designed for anomaly detection. It is grounded on the principle that anomalies are "few and different"—they occur infrequently and differ substantially from normal observations. Unlike numerous methods that initially characterize normal behavior and subsequently identify deviations, Isolation Forest directly identifies anomalies through a process of random isolation.

The algorithm operates through a combination of random tree generation, recursive partitioning, path length calculation, and anomaly scoring. This approach leverages a fundamental property of anomalies: they typically reside in sparse regions of the feature space, rendering them more amenable to isolation through random partitioning compared to normal instances clustered in dense regions.

Isolation Forest offers several advantages for behavioral anomaly detection. The algorithm exhibits linear scalability with data size and operates swiftly even on large datasets, enabling its application to systems with numerous agents. Unlike numerous methods, Isolation Forest does not presume specific data distributions or necessitate distance measures, rendering it robust across diverse behavioral data types. Analysts can discern the behavioral dimensions that drive anomalies by analyzing which features most frequently contribute to anomaly isolation. Furthermore, combining multiple random isolation trees mitigates sensitivity to individual feature selections and provides more stable anomaly rankings.

Applying Isolation Forest for behavioral fingerprinting entails several steps, including feature selection, contamination estimation, ensemble construction, threshold selection, and contextual interpretation. Isolation Forest has demonstrated effectiveness in diverse applications. In network security, it identifies unusual traffic patterns that may indicate intrusions. In financial compliance, it flags unusual transaction sequences potentially indicative of fraud. In industrial systems, it detects equipment behaviors that precede failures.

The method's primary limitations include challenges associated with extremely high-dimensional data (although feature selection can address this issue) and reduced effectiveness when anomalies cluster rather than appearing as isolated points. Despite these limitations, Isolation Forest remains one of the most widely applicable approaches for identifying behavioral anomalies in intricate systems.

On the other hand, One-Class Support Vector Machine (OCSVM) adopts a fundamentally distinct approach to anomaly detection, focusing on defining a boundary around normal behavior in feature space. Unlike supervised learning methods that necessitate labeled examples of both normal and anomalous instances, OCSVM learns solely from normal examples—a significant advantage when anomalies are scarce, diverse, or previously unrecognized.

The algorithm operates by mapping data to a high-dimensional feature space using kernel functions, finding the smallest hypersphere that contains most normal data points, defining a decision boundary that separates normal regions from outlier regions, and scoring new instances based on their position relative to this boundary. This approach effectively defines a "normal behavior region" in feature space, treating instances falling outside this region as potential anomalies.

For behavioral fingerprinting, OCSVM offers several advantages. The method precisely defines a boundary around normal behavior, identifying what constitutes "normal" behavioral patterns. Through kernel functions, OCSVM can handle non-linear relationships between behavioral features. The method can accommodate a small number of anomalies in training data through outlier tolerance parameters. Only support vectors (points near the decision boundary) need to be stored, enabling application to large-scale systems.

Implementing OCSVM for behavioral anomaly detection involves kernel selection, parameter tuning, training, threshold calibration, and monitoring. OCSVM has demonstrated effectiveness across numerous domains. In industrial control systems, it detects unusual sensor patterns indicating equipment malfunction. User behavior analytics identifies account behaviors deviating from established usage patterns. In autonomous vehicles, it recognizes unusual environmental conditions requiring human intervention.

The primary limitations of OCSVM include sensitivity to kernel and parameter selection, computational intensity for extremely large datasets, and challenges in capturing temporal anomalies without explicit feature engineering. Despite these constraints, OCSVM remains a potent tool for defining normal behavioral boundaries and identifying deviations that necessitate investigation.

Autoencoders constitute a neural network approach to anomaly detection, possessing distinctive advantages for behavioral fingerprinting. These networks are trained to reconstruct their input data after passing it through a bottleneck, thereby compelling the network to acquire efficient representations of typical patterns. Anomalies, being fundamentally distinct from training examples, typically generate higher reconstruction errors, thereby providing a natural mechanism for detection.

The autoencoder architecture consists of an encoder, decoder, and reconstruction error. For behavioral fingerprinting, this approach offers several notable advantages. In contrast to numerous methods that require manual feature engineering, autoencoders directly learn relevant behavioral representations from data. The neural network architecture can capture intricate nonlinear relationships between behavioral dimensions. The bottleneck layer provides a concise behavioral fingerprint encapsulating the essence of normal behavior. Contemporary implementations can effectively manage large-scale behavioral datasets with multiple features.

Implementing autoencoders for behavioral anomaly detection involves architecture design, training strategy, regularization selection, threshold determination, and refinement. Several autoencoder variants enhance anomaly detection capabilities.

Variational Autoencoders (VAEs) add probabilistic constraints to the latent space, producing more robust representations and enabling generative capabilities. Long Short-Term Memory Autoencoders (LSTM-AEs) incorporate recurrent structures to capture temporal dependencies in sequential behavioral data. Adversarial Autoencoders combine autoencoder training with adversarial mechanisms, improving representation quality and anomaly detection sensitivity.

Autoencoders have demonstrated particular effectiveness in complex behavioral domains. In network traffic analysis, they identify subtle attack patterns invisible to rule-based systems. In healthcare, they detect unusual patient trajectories indicating potential complications.

In the manufacturing industry, anomalous process sequences preceding quality issues are recognized.

The approach, however, encounters limitations, such as the substantial training data requirement, challenges in determining optimal network architectures, and the inherent "black box" nature of learned representations. Nevertheless, techniques like attention mechanisms and latent space visualization increasingly address interpretability concerns, rendering autoencoders an increasingly valuable tool for behavioral fingerprinting.

Understanding which behavioral features contribute most significantly to pattern detection and classification provides crucial insights for analytical interpretation and system intervention. Feature importance assessment techniques identify the most influential variables, enhancing model interpretability and guiding attention to the most significant behavioral dimensions.

Random Forests, a combination of multiple decision trees trained on random subsets of data and features, create an ensemble model[13] with superior performance and built-in feature importance metrics. This approach naturally quantifies the contribution of each feature to prediction accuracy, providing valuable insights into behavioral pattern drivers.

The Random Forest algorithm incorporates feature importance in several ways, including Mean Decrease in Impurity, Mean Decrease in Accuracy, and Minimal Depth. For behavioral fingerprinting, Random Forest feature importance offers several advantages. By averaging across numerous trees with diverse data and feature subsets, the method provides stable importance

---

[13] Ensemble models combine multiple learning algorithms to improve prediction performance beyond what any single model could achieve alone. They're a powerful approach in machine learning that often leads to more robust and accurate results.

rankings that are less susceptible to data noise. The approach captures feature importance even when relationships are highly non-linear or involve intricate interactions. Random Forests do not necessitate specific data distributions or structural assumptions, enabling their effective application across diverse behavioral data types. The feature importance metrics translate readily into comprehensible rankings that domain experts can validate and apply.

This methodology facilitates the identification of behavioral dimensions that most significantly distinguish various agent types or discern normal from anomalous behaviors. For instance, in financial transaction monitoring, Random Forest feature importance may reveal that transaction timing variance, counterparty diversity, and amount periodicity most strongly indicate fraudulent activity. In healthcare, it may demonstrate that medication adherence patterns, appointment regularity, and symptom reporting consistency are the most predictive factors of patient outcomes.

The primary limitations of Gradient Boosting include challenges with highly correlated features (where importance may be distributed across related variables) and potential biases toward high-cardinality features. These limitations can be addressed through correlation analysis and adjusted importance metrics.

Gradient Boosting is another ensemble approach that sequentially builds decision trees, with each tree focusing on correcting errors made by previous trees. Unlike Random Forests, which build independent trees in parallel, Gradient Boosting creates a sequential series of trees that progressively refine predictions. This approach provides particularly nuanced feature importance metrics that account for how features contribute to error reduction throughout the modeling process.

Gradient Boosting calculates feature importance through several mechanisms: split frequency, permutation importance, and SHAP[14] values. For behavioral fingerprinting, Gradient Boosting importance metrics offer distinct advantages. The boosting process reveals features contributing to increasingly subtle behavioral patterns not captured by initial trees. Importance metrics account for how features work together, identifying combinations that collectively distinguish behavioral patterns. Methods like SHAP values explain feature importance for individual predictions, revealing how the same feature may have different importance for different agent behaviors. Importance metrics directly relate to prediction improvement, providing calibrated measures of how much each feature contributes to model performance.

---

[14] SHAP (SHapley Additive exPlanations) values are a unified approach to explaining the output of any machine learning model. Based on cooperative game theory, SHAP values provide a mathematically sound method for attributing each feature's contribution to a specific prediction.

This approach has proven particularly valuable for complex behavioral domains where subtle patterns distinguish important categories.

In cybersecurity, Gradient Boosting importance metrics identify the telltale combinations of timing, volume, and access patterns that characterize sophisticated attacks. In customer analytics, they reveal how interaction sequence, sentiment progression, and timing collectively predict customer churn.

Gradient Boosting feature importance presents challenges, including computational intensity for large datasets, requirements for careful hyperparameter tuning, and sensitivity to noisy features. However, modern implementations increasingly address these limitations through algorithmic optimizations and regularization techniques.

The ultimate goal of behavioral fingerprinting is to develop concise, interpretable representations of how agents or systems operate—signatures that capture essential behavioral characteristics while filtering out noise and irrelevant variation. Creating and interpreting these fingerprints transform machine learning outputs into meaningful insights supporting human understanding and automated decision-making.

Complex behavioral patterns often involve dozens or hundreds of features, presenting challenges for human interpretation. Dimension reduction techniques transform high-dimensional behavioral data into lower-dimensional representations that preserve essential patterns while enabling visualization and interpretation.

Principal Component Analysis (PCA) identifies linear combinations of original features that capture the maximum variance. By projecting behavioral data onto these principal components, analysts can visualize the primary dimensions of variation in two or three dimensions. PCA aids in identifying behavioral clusters, outliers, and transitions that may be concealed in high-dimensional space.

T-Distributed Stochastic Neighbor Embedding (t-SNE) is a nonlinear dimensionality reduction technique that preserves local relationships between similar behaviors while allowing for larger distances between dissimilar ones. This approach is particularly effective in revealing cluster structures, especially when behavioral patterns manifest as complex manifolds in feature space.

In contrast, Uniform Manifold Approximation and Projection (UMAP) combines the advantages of t-SNE for preserving local relationships with enhanced preservation of global structure. This emerging technique often provides more stable visualizations that effectively maintain relative distances between behavioral clusters.

Autoencoders can simultaneously serve dual purposes: detecting anomalies and reducing dimensionality through their bottleneck layers. The learned latent representations often capture meaningful behavioral features that can be visualized and interpreted.

Effective dimension reduction visualization requires embedding stability, cluster validation, temporal tracking, and feature contribution mapping. These visualizations serve as powerful communication tools, enabling stakeholders to grasp complex behavioral patterns that would remain impenetrable in raw feature space. They support both exploratory analysis to discover unexpected patterns and confirmatory visualization to communicate established understandings.

Beyond visualization, behavioral fingerprinting requires constructing formalized profiles that characterize different agent types or states. These profiles serve as reference models for classification, anomaly detection, and system understanding.

Centroid-based profiles establish "typical" behavioral patterns for recognized groups. Following clustering, cluster centers in feature space represent prototypical behavior patterns for each group. These centroids can be transposed back to the original feature dimensions to generate interpretable descriptions of characteristic behaviors. For instance, a financial trader profile might specify typical trading frequencies, preferred asset classes, risk metrics, and temporal patterns.

Rule-based signatures discern decision rules that distinguish between behavioral categories. Decision tree ensembles and rule extraction algorithms identify conditional patterns that characterize distinct behaviors. These rules transform intricate statistical models into human-readable logic: "If feature A surpasses threshold X while feature B remains below threshold Y, then the behavior aligns with profile Z." Such explicit rules facilitate both comprehension and implementation in operational systems.

Statistical distribution models characterize behaviors through probability distributions rather than point estimates. These profiles define expected distributions for each behavioral feature, enabling probabilistic matching of new observations. This approach acknowledges natural variation within behavioral categories while still providing discriminative power.

Temporal sequence templates capture characteristic patterns of behavior over time. These templates may include typical event sequences, transition probabilities between states, or time-series motifs that recur within specific behavioral categories. Such temporal signatures prove particularly valuable for processes where the order and timing of actions carry significant meaning.

Effective behavioral profiles strike a balance between discriminative power, interpretability, robustness, and actionable insights. When meticulously constructed, behavioral profiles serve as reference models, supporting diverse analytical and operational functions. These functions encompass real-time classification of ongoing behaviors and strategic planning informed by behavioral comprehension.

Numerous intricate systems undergo behavioral evolution over time, with agents adapting strategies, learning from experience, or responding to environmental modifications. Capturing this temporal evolution is a pivotal aspect of comprehensive behavioral fingerprinting.

State transition modeling elucidates how agents traverse various behavioral states over time. Hidden Markov Models provide a natural framework for representing these transitions through their state transition matrices. Analysts gain insights into typical behavioral trajectories by analyzing these transition patterns, identifying catalysts that trigger state changes, and anticipating potential future state transitions.

Drift detection monitors the evolution of behavioral fingerprints over time, distinguishing between normal variations and significant shifts necessitating model updates. Techniques such as concept drift detection from machine learning can be applied to behavioral fingerprinting, automatically identifying instances where established behavioral models no longer accurately represent current patterns.

Intervention impact analysis evaluates the changes in behavioral patterns in response to specific interventions or environmental shifts. By comparing pre- and post-intervention fingerprints, analysts can assess the effectiveness of interventions, identify unforeseen adaptations, and refine future intervention strategies.

Cyclical pattern identification distinguishes between persistent evolutionary changes and cyclical patterns that recur at regular intervals. Fourier analysis, wavelet decomposition, and seasonal decomposition techniques assist in separating long-term trends from periodic oscillations, thereby enabling more accurate assessments of genuine evolutionary change.

Agent learning modeling elucidates how individual agents modify their behaviors in response to experience and feedback. Reinforcement learning frameworks can model how agents revise behavioral strategies in response to rewards and penalties, providing insights into adaptive processes that drive system evolution.

Temporal evolution analysis enhances behavioral fingerprinting by transforming static snapshots into a dynamic understanding. It reveals how behaviors adapt to changing conditions, how interventions trigger systemic responses, and how learning processes drive evolutionary trajectories of all crucial dimensions for comprehensively understanding complex adaptive systems.

As machine learning techniques become increasingly sophisticated, ensuring behavioral fingerprints remain interpretable presents significant challenges. Explainable AI (XAI) methods address this challenge by making complex model outputs comprehensible to human analysts, translating statistical patterns into meaningful insights.

Local Interpretable Model-agnostic Explanations (LIME) provides insights into individual predictions by approximating intricate models with simpler, interpretable models in the vicinity of specific instances. In the context of behavioral fingerprinting, LIME elucidates the reasons behind classifying specific behaviors into predefined categories or identifying anomalous patterns. It highlights the behavioral features that contributed to the classification decisions.

Shapley Additive explanations (SHAP) employ cooperative game theory principles to equitably distribute prediction credit among features. SHAP values elucidate the contribution of each behavioral feature to model outputs for both individual instances and across populations, offering both local and global interpretability.

Counterfactual explanations pinpoint the minimal alterations to behavioral features that would yield alternative classifications. These explanations address inquiries such as, "What modifications to this behavior would render it normal rather than suspicious?" Such counterfactuals provide actionable insights for intervention or behavioral modification.

Feature interaction visualization reveals how combinations of behavioral features jointly influence classifications beyond their individual effects. Techniques like partial dependence plots and accumulated local effects plots show how features work together, capturing interaction effects that simple feature importance rankings might miss.

Rule extraction distills intricate models into human-readable rule sets that approximate model behavior. Although these rules may not precisely capture all model intricacies, they offer interpretable approximations that domain experts can comprehend, validate, and apply.

When integrated into behavioral fingerprinting workflows, these XAI[15] techniques ensure that sophisticated machine learning models augment rather than obscure human comprehension. They transform opaque predictions into transparent, actionable insights that bridge statistical patterns to domain knowledge and operational decisions.

To demonstrate the practical application of behavioral fingerprinting techniques, let us analyze how these methods reveal concealed patterns in financial market trading behaviors. Financial markets exemplify classic instances of complex multi-agent systems, where numerous independent actors pursue diverse strategies while collectively determining market outcomes.

Our case study focuses on equity market trading, elucidating how distinct trader types can be identified through their behavioral signatures. The analysis integrates multiple data sources: transaction records, order book events, market environment data, and temporal indicators. The initial dataset encompassed over 50 million trading events from a six-month period, representing activities of approximately 10,000 distinct trading entities across multiple equity markets.

---

[15] Explainable AI refers to methods and techniques that allow humans to understand and interpret predictions made by machine learning models.

Raw trading data necessitated extensive preprocessing and feature engineering to extract behavioral signatures. This involved actor identification, temporal aggregation, feature extraction, and normalization. Initial analysis employed unsupervised learning to discern natural behavioral groupings without imposing prior classifications. This was achieved through dimensionality reduction, hierarchical clustering, DBSCAN analysis, and stability assessment.

This unsupervised approach identified eight distinct trader behavioral archetypes, each with distinctive characteristics that persisted across time periods and market conditions. The analysis generated detailed behavioral fingerprints for each identified trader type: high-frequency market makers, institutional block traders, momentum followers, contrarian liquidity providers, event-driven specialists, passive index replicators, statistical arbitrageurs, and technical pattern traders.

Beyond identifying established behavioral archetypes, anomaly detection techniques uncovered several categories of unusual trading behaviors: strategy transitions, hybrid behaviors, coordinated activities, and environmental anomalies. Isolation Forest demonstrated exceptional efficacy in identifying novel behavioral patterns deviating from established fingerprints, while autoencoders excelled in detecting subtle deviations from traders' established patterns.

Analyzing behavioral fingerprints over six months revealed several evolutionary patterns: adaptation cycles, environmental responses, competitive coevolution, and learning signatures. LSTM models proved particularly effective in capturing these temporal evolution patterns, identifying characteristic adaptation sequences that distinguish between different strategy types.

The behavioral fingerprinting approach has yielded several valuable applications, including market monitoring, risk management, strategy development, and market simulation.

This case study illustrates how behavioral fingerprinting techniques can transform vast, intricate behavioral datasets into discernible patterns that augment system comprehension and facilitate more effective intervention, monitoring, and prediction.

Behavioral fingerprinting employing machine learning presents a potent methodology for comprehending intricate multi-agent systems. By identifying distinctive patterns in the behavior of agents, constructing interpretable representations of these patterns, and monitoring their temporal evolution, these techniques render overwhelming behavioral complexity into comprehensible insights that support both understanding and action.

The techniques we have explored reveal natural groupings within behavioral data, capture temporal patterns that characterize the unfolding of behaviors over time, identify unusual behaviors that may signify emerging threats or innovations, and assist in determining which behavioral dimensions contribute to pattern recognition. Collectively, these techniques facilitate the creation of comprehensive behavioral fingerprints—unique signature patterns that distinguish various agent types, operational states, or strategic approaches.

In the subsequent chapter, we will leverage behavioral fingerprinting insights to delve into agent-based modeling—techniques that simulate interactions between agents with distinct behavioral fingerprints to comprehend how micro-level behaviors manifest in macro-level system outcomes. This modeling approach enables the exploration of hypothetical scenarios, testing potential interventions before implementation, and investigating how systems might respond to evolving conditions or novel challenges.

CHAPTER 5

Modeling Complex Systems

While behavioral fingerprinting techniques are effective in identifying patterns in empirical data, they primarily provide descriptive rather than causal insights. To truly comprehend how individual agent behaviors collectively produce system-level outcomes and predict how systems might respond to novel conditions or interventions, we require computational models that can simulate these intricate interaction dynamics. Agent-based modeling (ABM) precisely fulfills this requirement, providing virtual laboratories where theories about multi-agent systems can be tested, refined, and applied.

Agent-based modeling represents a fundamentally distinct approach from traditional equation-based modeling. In contrast to attempting to describe system behavior through aggregate mathematical relationships, ABM simulates the actions and interactions of autonomous agents, enabling system-level patterns to emerge naturally from these micro-level behaviors. This approach aligns seamlessly with complex systems composed of independent actors, each pursuing individual objectives while collectively contributing to broader system dynamics.

This chapter delves into the design, implementation, and validation of agent-based models for complex systems analysis. It elucidates how behavioral fingerprints ascertained through empirical analysis can guide realistic agent specifications, how to define interaction rules governing agent relationships, how to design environments that influence agent behaviors, and how to validate simulation results against real-world data. Subsequently, it explores how these validated models can serve as experimental testbeds for elucidating causal mechanisms and evaluating potential interventions.

Designing Agents Based on Behavioral Fingerprints

The foundation of effective agent-based modeling lies in creating agent specifications that realistically capture the behavioral characteristics of their real-world counterparts. The behavioral fingerprinting techniques discussed in the previous chapter provide empirically grounded templates for these specifications, enabling models grounded in observed reality rather than theoretical assumptions.

From Fingerprints to Agent Specifications

Translating behavioral fingerprints into agent specifications involves a series of fundamental steps. The initial step involves attribute definition, which entails ascertaining the specific characteristics that agents must possess to manifest the observed behavioral patterns. These attributes encompass a range of entities, including state variables, internal conditions that influence agent decisions and evolve over time. These state variables encompass resources, knowledge, preferences, and strategies. Additionally, perception capabilities encompass the information from the environment and other agents that is accessible to the agent. Decision mechanisms encompass the processes through which agents process available information to select actions. Learning parameters encompass the mechanisms through which agents modify their behavior in response to experience and outcomes. Finally, constraint factors encompass limitations on agent capabilities, resources, or actions.

The second step involves behavioral rule extraction: developing algorithmic representations of decision processes that replicate observed behaviors. These rules can take various forms, including condition-action rules (simple if-then logic that triggers specific actions when conditions are met), utility functions (mathematical formulations that agents seek to maximize or minimize), decision trees (hierarchical choice structures reflecting sequential decision processes), neural network models (data-driven decision mechanisms trained on observed behaviors), and probabilistic response functions (stochastic models capturing the likelihood of different responses to given conditions).

The third step is heterogeneity implementation: incorporating variations between agents to reflect observed diversity in real-world behaviors. This heterogeneity can be implemented through parameter distribution (assigning attribute values drawn from empirically derived statistical distributions), agent classes (creating distinct agent types corresponding to different behavioral fingerprint clusters), individual learning trajectories (implementing unique adaptation paths for each agent), network position variation (differentiating agents based on their relationship structures), and historical path dependence (allowing past experiences to uniquely shape each agent's current behavior).

The sophistication of agent specifications should match the complexity required to reproduce observed behaviors while maintaining computational feasibility. In some cases, relatively simple rule-based agents may suffice to capture essential dynamics. More complex cognitive architectures incorporating learning, planning, and adaptation mechanisms may be necessary in others.

Cognitive Architectures for Realistic Agents

Implementing suitable cognitive architectures becomes paramount for systems where agent cognition plays a substantial role in determining behavioral outcomes. These architectures serve as structured frameworks for organizing cognitive processes that govern how agents perceive, make decisions, and execute actions.

The Belief-Desire-Intention (BDI) Architecture organizes agent cognition into three fundamental components: beliefs (the agent's informational state and its understanding of the world), desires (the agent's motivational state and its objectives), and intentions (the agent's deliberative state and its committed plans). This architecture serves as a natural framework for developing goal-directed agents with practical reasoning capabilities. In financial market modeling, for instance, a trader agent could maintain beliefs about market conditions, desires for profit targets and risk limits, and intentions representing specific trading strategies currently in execution.

Recognition-Primed Decision (RPD) Models employ expertise-based decision-making, wherein agents recognize situations based on their experience, retrieve associated actions that have proven effective in similar situations, mentally simulate the outcomes of these actions before execution, and execute the selected actions, observing the results. This approach effectively models expert decision-making in domains where pattern recognition and experience-based responses predominate. For instance, emergency responder agents in crisis simulations may utilize RPD processes to swiftly identify situation types and deploy appropriate response protocols.

Learning Classifier Systems (LCS) implement adaptive rule-based decision-making, where rules are composed of condition-action pairs. These rules compete for activation based on fitness measures, with successful rules receiving reinforcement. New rules are generated through genetic algorithms or other evolutionary processes. This architecture naturally models agents that learn through experience, gradually enhancing their behavior through trial and error. Market participants learning to identify profitable opportunities or consumers navigating complex choice environments can be effectively modeled using LCS approaches.

Neural Network Agents utilize trained neural networks to map from situational inputs to behavioral outputs. These data-driven decision mechanisms can capture intricate, non-linear relationships between environmental conditions and agent responses without explicitly formulating rules. When substantial behavioral data is available, but underlying decision rules remain opaque, neural network agents provide a practical modeling approach.

The selection of appropriate cognitive architectures should be guided by both empirical evidence regarding how real-world agents make decisions and the specific research questions the model aims to address. While highly sophisticated cognitive models may enhance realism, they also introduce additional parameters that require calibration and validation.

Balancing Sophistication with Parsimony

A persistent challenge in agent specification is balancing behavioral complexity and model parsimony. While more intricate agent specifications may enhance realism, they also introduce additional parameters, computational demands, and the potential for overfitting. Several guiding principles facilitate this equilibrium.

The Requisite Complexity Principle posits that agent specifications should be limited to the level of complexity necessary to replicate the behavioral patterns pertinent to research inquiries. Unnecessary complexity should be eschewed unless explicitly justified. The Incremental Elaboration Approach recommends commencing with relatively simple agent specifications and incrementally introducing complexity only when simpler models prove inadequate in reproducing observed patterns. This approach facilitates the identification of the minimal necessary complexity.

The Behavioral Validation Focus prioritizes reproducing observable behaviors by agent specifications over speculating about unobservable internal processes. Different internal mechanisms can produce identical external behaviors; therefore, models should focus on the observable aspects. Furthermore, the Sensitivity Analysis Requirement acknowledges that more complex agent specifications necessitate more extensive sensitivity analysis to comprehend parameter interactions and identify potential vulnerabilities in model behavior.

> By judiciously balancing sophistication with parsimony, modelers can construct agent specifications that encapsulate fundamental behavioral characteristics while ensuring computational tractability and analytical clarity.

Defining Interaction Rules

While agent specifications define individual behavioral tendencies, interaction rules govern how agents influence one another's states, decisions, and actions. These rules establish the relational fabric of the multi-agent system, shaping how individual behaviors aggregate into collective outcomes.

Types of Agent Interactions

Agent-based models can incorporate various interaction types, capturing distinct relationship dimensions within intricate systems. Direct Exchange Interactions entail explicit transfers between agents, encompassing resource exchanges (transferring assets, goods, or services), information sharing (communicating knowledge, beliefs, or signals), and collaborative actions (joint endeavors necessitating coordinated participation). These interactions typically involve explicit agent decisions regarding engagement, although they may be subject to constraints such as proximity, network connectivity, or institutional regulations.

Indirect environmental interactions occur when agents influence one another by modifying shared environments. These interactions encompass resource competition, where agents consume limited resources that become unavailable to others; environmental modification, where agents alter the environmental conditions experienced by others; and stigmergy, where agents leave environmental traces that influence others' subsequent behavior. These interactions can transpire without direct agent awareness of others, yet they still establish substantial interdependencies that shape system dynamics.

Network-mediated interactions depend on relationship structures that determine interaction possibilities, including fixed networks (predetermined relationship structures that constrain interaction possibilities), dynamic networks (evolving relationship structures that agents can modify through their actions), and multiplex networks (multiple relationship types operating simultaneously between agents). Network structures may significantly influence system outcomes by determining who can interact with whom, potentially creating information bottlenecks, opinion clusters, or resource distribution patterns.

Normative interactions encompass social influences on an agent's behavior, including social learning (observing and imitating others' actions), norm emergence (the development of shared behavioral expectations), reputation systems (evaluating agents based on their past behavior histories), and identity formation (group membership influencing individual behavioral tendencies). These interactions extend beyond simple exchanges to encompass how an agent's social context shapes their behavior, potentially leading to cultural evolution, conformity pressures, or cooperative institutions.

Empirical knowledge regarding how real-world agents influence one another within the modeled system should guide the selection of suitable interaction mechanisms. Many intricate systems involve multiple interaction types operating concurrently, necessitating models that integrate diverse relationship dimensions.

Environmental Design and Simulation Methodologies

While agents and their interactions form the core of agent-based models, the environment within which these agents operate provides essential context that shapes behaviors and outcomes. Environmental design involves specifying both the structural characteristics of the space agents inhabit and the dynamic processes that modify this space over time.

Types of Environments

Agent-based models can utilize diverse environments, each tailored to specific modeling scenarios. Cellular Grid Environments partition space into discrete cells, each with distinct characteristics. These environments offer intuitive spatial representation, elucidating neighborhood connections. They facilitate efficient computational execution through array structures, naturally embody geographic spaces with location-specific attributes, and support visualization through color-coded grid displays. Cellular environments prove particularly valuable for models where spatial interactions substantially impact system dynamics, encompassing urban development, ecosystem interactions, and disease propagation.

Continuous Space Environments represent locations as coordinates in n-dimensional space, enabling precise positioning without cell-based limitations. They facilitate continuous movement in any direction, accommodate variable interaction distances, and provide a more realistic depiction of physical systems. These environments are particularly advantageous for systems where precise distances are critical, as artificial grid boundaries would introduce unrealistic constraints.

Network Environments represent spatial relationships topologically rather than geographically, emphasizing connection patterns over physical distances. These environments directly capture relationship structures without spatial metaphors, representing abstract spaces such as information networks or organizational structures. They enable efficient modeling of systems where physical space plays a minimal role and support analysis of how network topology influences system dynamics. Network environments naturally model systems organized around relationships rather than geographic proximity, encompassing diverse domains such as social media, corporate hierarchies, and academic citation networks.

Abstract Feature Spaces represent environments as multidimensional attribute spaces rather than physical or network structures. In these environments, agent positions represent attribute combinations rather than physical locations. "Distance" represents similarity along specified dimensions, regions may have different densities, constraints, or resource distributions, and movement represents change in attributes rather than physical relocation. These environments effectively model systems organized around conceptual rather than physical relationships, such as product feature spaces, political ideology landscapes, or cultural attribute domains.

Most sophisticated agent-based models carefully select appropriate environment types based on the specific systems being modeled. Sometimes, multiple environment representations are simultaneously implemented to capture different relationship dimensions.

Resource Dynamics

Many intricate systems involve agents competing for, consuming, and producing resources within shared environments. Modeling resource dynamics necessitates specifying the distribution of resources, their regeneration or depletion processes, and how agents access and utilize them.

Resource Distribution Patterns dictate how resources are allocated across the environment. They encompass uniform distribution (resources evenly distributed throughout the environment), patchy distribution (resources concentrated in specific regions), gradient-based distribution (resource density following continuous gradients), and network-mediated distribution (resources traversing network structures). These distribution patterns profoundly influence agent movement, competition dynamics, and territorial behaviors.

Resource Regeneration Mechanisms outline how depleted resources are replenished over time. These mechanisms encompass various types of regeneration, including constant rate regeneration, where resources replenish at fixed rates irrespective of their current levels; density-dependent growth, where regeneration rates vary proportionally to the current resource density; seasonal variation, characterized by cyclical changes in regeneration rates; and event-triggered replenishment, where resources are renewed in response to specific environmental events. Implementing these regeneration mechanisms generates temporal dynamics that agents must adapt to, potentially leading to boom-bust cycles, sustainable harvesting strategies, or competitive exclusion.

Agent-Resource Interaction Rules govern the behavior of agents in locating, accessing, and utilizing resources. These rules encompass perception mechanisms (how agents detect resources within their environment), acquisition strategies (how agents claim or extract resources they have identified), consumption models (how acquired resources are transformed into agent benefits), efficiency parameters (how effectively agents extract value from resources), and storage capabilities (how agents maintain resource reserves for future utilization). These rules establish competitive advantages among different agent types, determine the potential for resource monopolization, and facilitate the emergence of specialized resource utilization strategies.

Resource Conversion Networks (RCNs) model the transformation of resources from one type to another, encompassing production chains (sequences converting raw materials into intermediate and final products), by-product generation (secondary resources created through primary resource processing), recycling loops (conversion of waste back into usable resources), and efficiency tradeoffs (relationships between resource inputs and outputs). These networks facilitate the modeling of intricate economic systems characterized by specialized production, exchange relationships, and supply chain dynamics.

Through the meticulous design of resource dynamics, modelers can construct environments that accurately represent the opportunity structures, constraints, and temporal patterns that influence the behaviors of agents in resource-dependent systems.

Simulation and Validation Methodologies

The development of agent specifications, interaction rules, and environmental designs constitutes the foundation of an agent-based model. However, the true test lies in assessing how these components interact to yield system-level behaviors. Simulation methodologies serve as the means to execute these models, while validation approaches ensure that model outcomes accurately reflect real-world dynamics.

Validation Against Real-World Data

While agent-based models inevitably involve simplifications and abstractions, their value for comprehending real-world systems hinges on establishing reliable connections between model behaviors and empirical realities. Validation methodologies establish these connections through systematic comparisons with observational or experimental data.

Pattern-Oriented Modeling (POM) aims to simultaneously replicate multiple empirical patterns by identifying characteristic patterns in the real system at various levels and scales. It develops model versions with alternative agent specifications and interaction rules, tests which versions successfully replicate multiple patterns simultaneously, and retains models that generate the complete pattern set while discarding those that fail. This approach recognizes that multiple model configurations may reproduce a single pattern, but far fewer can simultaneously reproduce multiple patterns across different scales and conditions.

Parameter Calibration involves systematically adjusting model parameters to optimize alignment with empirical data by identifying empirically observable metrics corresponding to model outputs. It defines objective functions measuring the discrepancy between model and empirical metrics, applies optimization algorithms to identify parameter combinations minimizing discrepancies, and validates calibrated models against data not used in the calibration process. Calibration approaches encompass manual adjustments guided by domain expertise and automated methods such as genetic algorithms, simulated annealing, or Bayesian optimization.

Comprehensive validation typically integrates multiple approaches, establishing model credibility through convergent evidence from various validation methods rather than relying solely on any single validation technique.

Case Study: Simulating Market Dynamics

To illustrate the practical application of agent-based modeling techniques, let us examine a case study involving financial market simulation. This case study demonstrates how empirically-derived behavioral fingerprints can inform agent specifications, how interaction rules can capture market mechanisms, and how simulation results can be validated against real-world market behaviors.

The market simulation model integrated multiple components to create a realistic yet computationally tractable representation of equity market dynamics.

The agent population consisted of various trader types, each characterized by distinct behavioral fingerprints identified through empirical analysis. These trader types included high-frequency market makers employing bid-ask spread strategies with rapid order adjustments, institutional block traders executing large orders with strategic timing to minimize market impact, momentum followers trading in the direction of recent price movements with acceleration/deceleration rules, contrarian liquidity providers taking positions against short-term price movements, event-driven specialists responding to specific market events according to characteristic patterns, and passive index replicators trading to maintain portfolios aligned with benchmark indices. Each agent type was implemented with specification parameters derived from empirical fingerprints, encompassing activity frequencies, position sizing rules, risk management constraints, and strategic adaptation mechanisms.

The model was implemented using a hybrid approach, integrating a specialized order book engine with Python-based agent implementations. Simulation execution followed a structured process involving initialization, execution, and analysis phases. The model underwent rigorous validation, comparing simulation outputs with empirical market data across multiple dimensions. This validation included statistical property validation, microstructure pattern validation, agent composition experiments, and event response validation.

The validated market simulation has enabled numerous valuable applications, including market design analysis, regulatory impact assessment, risk management scenario testing, and strategy development. The case study illustrates how agent-based modeling provides inaccessible insights through equation-based models or statistical analysis alone. By explicitly modeling heterogeneous agent behaviors, their interactions through market mechanisms, and their adaptive responses to changing conditions, the simulation captured emergent market dynamics that more aggregated approaches would overlook.

Conclusion

Agent-based modeling provides a robust approach for comprehending intricate systems composed of independent entities pursuing distinct objectives. By meticulously designing agents based on empirically derived behavioral characteristics, defining realistic interaction protocols, constructing suitable environmental structures, and validating simulations against empirical data, we can construct virtual laboratories that offer causal insights into system dynamics.

In contrast to purely statistical approaches that identify patterns without elucidating mechanisms, or equation-based models that obscure individual heterogeneity, agent-based models elucidate how system-level behaviors emerge from micro-level interactions among diverse agents. This approach proves particularly advantageous for systems characterized by heterogeneity, adaptation, and the emergence of unpredictable phenomena from component interactions.

The agent-based modeling process fosters a mutually reinforcing cycle with behavioral fingerprinting. Empirical fingerprinting provides realistic templates for agent specifications, while simulation outcomes identify the behavioral dimensions that most significantly influence system outcomes, guiding further empirical investigation. This iterative dialogue between empirical analysis and computational modeling establishes a robust framework for advancing our comprehension of complex systems.

CHAPTER 6

Game Theory Applications for Strategic Interactions

While agent-based modeling provides a robust framework for simulating intricate systems, game theory offers complementary analytical tools specifically designed for comprehending strategic interactions. Agent-based models excel at capturing emergent patterns from numerous interactions, whereas game theory provides formal structures for analyzing the fundamental logic of strategic decision-making. By integrating game-theoretic approaches into our broader analytical framework, we acquire enhanced capabilities for modeling conflicts and collaborative opportunities between subgroups within complex systems.

Game theory's unique strength lies in its capacity to formalize the strategic interdependence among decision-makers, situations where each actor's optimal choice is contingent upon the choices made by others. This interdependence is prevalent in numerous critical interactions within complex systems, encompassing market competition, resource allocation, and coalition formation. By meticulously modeling these strategic dynamics, game theory facilitates predicting probable outcomes, identifies potential intervention points, and devises mechanisms that harmonize individual incentives with collective objectives.

Game Formulation for Subgroup Interaction

The initial step in applying game theory to intricate systems involves formulating suitable game representations of strategic interactions among subgroups. This process necessitates identifying the participants, their available strategies, the payoffs associated with various strategy combinations, and the information structures that influence decision-making processes.

In complex systems, determining the appropriate players for game-theoretic analysis requires careful consideration of system structure and research objectives.

When analyzing interactions between distinct behavioral clusters identified through fingerprinting, each subgroup can be treated as a unified player. This approach proves valuable when subgroups exhibit coherent decision-making patterns and internal coordination, allowing simplified representation as singular strategic entities.

Modeling individual agents as players may be necessary in systems where individual heterogeneity and internal subgroup dynamics significantly influence outcomes. This more granular approach captures strategic diversity within subgroups but increases model complexity and computational requirements.

Many complex systems involve dynamic coalition formation, where players form alliances that act collectively. Coalitional game theory provides frameworks for analyzing which coalitions are likely to form and how they distribute benefits among members.

Systems with nested organizational structures may require multi-level game formulations, where players at one level engage in games constrained by the outcomes of games at other levels. These models capture how strategic interactions within organizational units influence interactions between units.

The appropriate player definition depends on the system's actual decision-making structure and the specific research questions being addressed. In certain instances, comparative analysis employing alternative player definitions may offer complementary insights into the operational dynamics of strategic dynamics across diverse system levels.

Strategy Space Definition

Strategies encompass the choices available to players within a game. Defining suitable strategy spaces necessitates a delicate balance between realism and analytical tractability, ensuring that strategically important options are adequately represented.

Firstly, identify the fundamental actions available to each player through empirical observation, system rules, or theoretical considerations. These actions serve as the foundation of strategies.

Secondly, define strategies as either pure strategies (specific action choices for each decision point), mixed strategies (probability distributions over available actions), sequential strategies (contingent plans specifying actions based on game history), or behavioral strategies (decision rules mapping information states to action probabilities).

The potential strategy space may be extensive for intricate systems. Effective formulation necessitates identifying strategically equivalent options that can be consolidated, prioritizing strategically significant dimensions while abstracting less critical details, and employing parametric representations to capture strategy families with manageable parameters.

Define strategy spaces based on observed behaviors rather than theoretical possibilities when possible.

Behavioral fingerprinting analysis can identify the actual strategy space utilized by system participants, significantly reducing dimensionality while maintaining realism.

Well-constructed strategy spaces capture the essential strategic options without becoming unmanageably complex. They should include strategies actually observed in the system, while potentially incorporating innovative strategies not yet implemented but theoretically viable.

Payoff Structure Modeling

Payoffs represent the outcomes that players receive from various strategy combinations. Accurate payoff modeling is essential for meaningful game-theoretic analysis.

Firstly, determine what players are actually optimizing. This may include economic returns (profits, resource acquisition, market share), positional advantages (competitive standing, territorial control), risk management (uncertainty reduction, survival probability), or mixed objectives with varying weights.

When feasible, estimate payoffs from observed outcomes through historical performance data under different strategy combinations, experimental results from controlled strategic interactions, or stakeholder assessments of relative outcome values.

For intricate interdependencies, construct mathematical functions that compute payoffs contingent upon player strategies, environmental conditions, resource limitations, and interaction mechanisms.

When outcomes are uncertain, payoffs utilize expected utility calculations, risk-adjusted valuation models, prospect-theoretic formulations that account for cognitive biases, or robust payoff ranges that acknowledge fundamental uncertainty.

For extended interactions, address intertemporal aspects through discounted future payoffs, state-dependent continuation values, or finite-horizon terminal conditions.

Payoff structures should reflect the incentives driving player decisions while capturing the interdependencies creating strategic tension. When feasible, validate payoff models against observed choices to ensure they accurately represent player motivations.

Information Structure Specification

Information structures significantly influence player decision-making processes. These structures fundamentally shape strategic reasoning and often generate substantial complexities in game-theoretic analysis:

- **Complete Information**: All players possess complete knowledge of the full payoff structure.

- **Incomplete Information**: Players have uncertainty regarding certain payoff-relevant factors.
- **Perfect Information:** All previous moves are observable.
- **Imperfect Information**: Some previous moves remain undisclosed.
- **Symmetric Information**: All players have equal access to the same information.
- **Asymmetric Information**: Some players possess information that others lack.

Demonstrate how players acquire information during gameplay through active investigation processes, drawing insights from observed actions, facilitating information exchange through signaling or communication, or making informed decisions based on information acquisition or investment.

Define "commonly known" information, which is widely understood among players, as this higher-order knowledge plays a crucial role in strategic reasoning.

Realistic information structures often exhibit substantial complexity, with players possessing partial and asymmetric information that undergoes evolution throughout the interaction. Game formulations should effectively capture fundamental informational constraints while maintaining analytical tractability.

Game Type Selection

Different strategic contexts necessitate distinct game formulations. Selecting the appropriate game type ensures that the model accurately captures the fundamental characteristics of the interaction being investigated:

- **Normal Form Games** offer the simplest formulation for analyzing strategic interdependence without temporal dynamics—single-stage games where players simultaneously select strategies.

- **Extensive Form Games** capture the temporal progression of strategic interactions. They are multi-stage games in which players make sequential decisions, potentially with incomplete information regarding previous moves.

- **Repeated Games** model interactions that occur multiple times with the same players, potentially enabling reputation effects and the emergence of complex conditional strategies.

- **Stochastic Games** represent interactions in which the game structure evolves according to probabilistic transitions, creating dynamic strategic environments.

- **Bayesian Games** explicitly model player uncertainty about game parameters, necessitating the analysis of how beliefs and information influence strategic choices.

- **Cooperative Games** focus on coalition formation and value distribution rather than specific strategic choices suitable for analyzing collaborative possibilities.

- **Evolutionary Games** analyze the prevalence of strategies in populations where successful strategies replicate more frequently, without assuming rationality.

- **Differential Games** employ continuous-time models, wherein players manipulate state variables through differential equations. These models are particularly useful for scenarios involving resource competition or pursuit-evasion dynamics.

The selection of the appropriate game type hinges on the temporal structure, information characteristics, and strategic objectives of the interaction being modeled. Complex systems frequently comprise interconnected games of diverse types, necessitating integrated analysis across game formulations.

Equilibrium Analysis

Once games are meticulously formulated, equilibrium analysis assists in identifying stable outcomes that may emerge from strategic interactions. Equilibrium concepts serve as solution criteria for predicting probable behavior when players act strategically in response to one another.

Nash Equilibria and Extensions

The Nash equilibrium concept forms the cornerstone of non-cooperative game theory, identifying strategy combinations where no player can gain an advantage by unilaterally altering their strategy:

- **Pure Strategy Nash Equilibria** exists when players' deterministic strategy choices form stable combinations. Identifying these equilibria entails determining strategy profiles where each strategy best responds to others' choices. Although conceptually simple, many games lack pure strategy equilibria or contain multiple equilibria, posing prediction challenges.

- **Mixed Strategy Nash Equilibria** involves probability distributions over available strategies, with each player's mixture rendering others indifferent between their pure strategy. These equilibria are always present in finite games but may yield counterintuitive predictions, particularly when interpreted as deliberate randomization rather than population frequency distributions.

Refinements to the basic Nash equilibrium address its limitations by incorporating additional criteria. These criteria include Subgame Perfect Equilibrium (which necessitates Nash equilibrium behavior in every subgame, thereby eliminating non-credible threats), Perfect Bayesian Equilibrium (which combines sequential rationality with consistent belief updating via Bayes' rule), Trembling Hand Perfect Equilibrium (which requires stability against small mistake probabilities), and Proper Equilibrium (which imposes a rationality hierarchy on mistakes).

Computational approaches are indispensable for identifying equilibria in intricate games, such as linear complementarity programs for bimatrix games, the Lemke-Howson algorithm for two-player games, support enumeration methods for games with manageable strategy spaces, and approximation algorithms for games that are too complex to yield an exact solution.

Equilibrium analysis offers pivotal insights into probable stable outcomes of strategic interactions, enabling the prediction of system behavior when participants act rationally in response to others' choices. However, these predictions necessitate meticulous interpretation, particularly when applied to complex systems where participants may not fully optimize or may pursue objectives that deviate from those explicitly modeled.

Pareto Optimality and Collective Outcomes

While Nash equilibria identify individually stable outcomes, Pareto optimality addresses collective efficiency—whether outcomes could be improved for some participants without harming others.

An outcome is Pareto optimal if no other outcome exists that would make at least one player better off without making any player worse off. This concept facilitates the identification of collectively desirable outcomes that are independent of strategic stability.

Numerous games present fundamental conflicts between individual interests and collective outcomes, resulting in Nash equilibria that are Pareto suboptimal. Classic examples include the Prisoner's Dilemma, where mutual defection leads to worse outcomes for both parties compared to mutual cooperation; the Tragedy of the Commons, where resource overexploitation reduces total value extraction; and Arms Races, where mutual armament consumes resources that could benefit all parties.

Several metrics quantify the disparity between equilibrium outcomes and optimal results, including the Price of Anarchy (the ratio between the worst equilibrium outcome and the social optimum), the Price of Stability (the ratio between the best equilibrium outcome and the social optimum), and Efficiency Loss (the absolute difference between the equilibrium and optimal outcomes).

When equilibrium outcomes are substantially suboptimal, mechanism design provides systematic methodologies for modifying game structures to align individual incentives with collective objectives. These approaches may encompass establishing property rights to internalize externalities, implementing tax or subsidy systems that incorporate social costs and benefits, the design of information revelation mechanisms that address asymmetric information, or creating commitment devices that facilitate cooperative solutions.

Understanding the relationship between strategic equilibria and Pareto efficiency facilitates the identification of situations where intervention can enhance system outcomes. This knowledge guides mechanism design efforts to maximize collective results while acknowledging strategic realities.

Evolutionary Stable Strategies

In systems where strategies are disseminated through imitation, replication, or selection rather than rational optimization, evolutionary game theory offers alternative equilibrium concepts centered on stability under evolutionary dynamics.

An Evolutionary Stable Strategy (ESS) is a strategy that, when adopted by a population, cannot be invaded by a small number of mutants employing an alternative strategy.

Formally, a strategy S* is evolutionary stable if

1. $(S^*, S^*) \geq (S, S^*)$ for all alternative strategies S (Nash equilibrium condition).
2. If $(S^*, S^*) = (S, S^*)$, then $(S^*, S) > (S, S)$ (stability against neutral mutations).

Replicator Dynamics are mathematical models describing how strategy frequencies evolve over time based on relative performance. The differential equation governing this process is

$$dx\_i/dt = x\_i[(Ax)\_i: x^T Ax]$$

where x_i represents the frequency of strategy i, A is the payoff matrix, and $(Ax)_i$ denotes the expected payoff to strategy i against the current population.

Risk Dominance analyzes the evolutionary equilibrium that is more probable to emerge when multiple equilibria coexist. A strategy is considered risk-dominant if it outperforms its alternatives against a diverse population.

Stochastic Stability identifies the states most likely to persist in the face of continuous, small random perturbations affecting the system, offering more accurate predictions for long-term outcomes.

Evolutionary stability concepts prove particularly valuable in analyzing systems where participants learn through imitation rather than optimization, where strategies are transmitted through cultural or biological means, where selection pressures shape strategy distributions, or where bounded rationality limits direct calculation of optimal responses.

These approaches connect game-theoretic thinking with evolutionary processes, providing powerful tools for understanding emergent behavioral patterns in complex adaptive systems where strategic behaviors evolve rather than being consciously designed.

Simulation, Scenario Analysis, and Strategic Applications

While analytical equilibrium concepts offer valuable insights, numerous intricate games defy complete mathematical solutions due to their substantial size, complexity, or stochastic nature. Simulation approaches, in contrast, complement analytical methods by computationally exploring game dynamics, thereby uncovering patterns and outcomes that may remain concealed in purely mathematical analysis.

Game Simulation Methodologies

Several methodologies enable computational exploration of game dynamics beyond analytical solutions:

- **Agent-Based Game Simulation (ABGS)** integrates game-theoretic interactions within agent-based modeling frameworks. Agents execute predefined strategies or decision rules, interactions adhere to the game's structure, outcomes accumulate over multiple interactions, and strategies adapt based on performance feedback. This approach seamlessly combines game theory with the agent-based modeling techniques outlined in Chapter 5, establishing a comprehensive framework for strategic analysis in intricate systems.

- **Evolutionary Algorithm Approaches** employ genetic programming or evolutionary computation techniques to strategy spaces. Initial strategy populations are generated randomly or from observed behaviors. Strategies compete based on game performance, and successful strategies reproduce with variation (mutation/crossover). Populations evolve toward effective strategic profiles. These approaches reveal which strategies emerge from evolutionary processes without assuming rationality, providing insights into adaptive strategy development in complex environments.

- **Monte Carlo Methods**[16] employ probabilistic game outcomes through repeated random sampling. Random strategy profiles are generated according to specified distributions, game outcomes are computed for each profile, and the results are aggregated to characterize outcome distributions. Sensitivity analysis reveals how parameter variations affect distributions. These methods prove particularly valuable for games with stochastic elements or where mixed strategies play significant roles.

- **Learning Model Simulations** employ specific models that elucidate how players acquire knowledge through experience. These encompass reinforcement learning approaches that modify strategy probabilities in accordance with actual payoffs, belief-based models that revise expectations regarding others' strategies based on observations, experience-weighted attraction models that amalgamate reinforcement and belief learning, and neural network models that implement adaptive decision processes devoid of predetermined structures. These simulations elucidate the evolution of strategic behavior through learning processes, potentially unveiling patterns divergent from equilibrium predictions derived from ideal rationality.

---

[16] Monte Carlo models are computational algorithms that rely on repeated random sampling to obtain numerical results. The core concept is to use randomness to solve problems that might be deterministic in principle.

> *By integrating these simulation methodologies with analytical approaches, researchers can better comprehend strategic dynamics within intricate systems. This enables the identification of both theoretical equilibrium points and probable evolutionary trajectories.*

One of the most valuable applications of game theory involves systematically exploring hypothetical scenarios through counterfactual analysis. This approach enables the understanding of how alterations in game parameters impact strategic outcomes:

- **Structural Variation Analysis** examines how modifying the game structure influences results by introducing or eliminating available strategies, altering the decision sequence, modifying information structures, or altering the number or composition of players. These variations reveal the sensitivity of outcomes to specific game structures, identifying which structural elements are critical determinants of results.

- **Payoff Modification Scenarios** analyze the impact of altering incentives on strategic behavior by introducing taxes, subsidies, or penalties, resource or capability reallocation, risk-reward relationship modification, or temporal discounting structure alterations. These scenarios facilitate the design of intervention strategies capable of inducing equilibria toward more favorable outcomes.

- **Information Structure Experiments** investigate the influence of information dissemination on strategic decisions by implementing transparency requirements, establishing certification or verification systems, creating information aggregation mechanisms, or modifying communication channels. These experiments elucidate the role of information availability in shaping strategic behavior, potentially identifying informational interventions that enhance outcomes.

- **Environmental Condition Variations** investigate the impact of external factors on game outcomes, particularly resource availability and scarcity, competitive intensity, regulatory changes, and technological advancements. These variations provide insights into the evolution of strategic interactions in response to changing environmental conditions, enabling the development of robust strategies or policy designs.

- **Systematic Counterfactual Exploration** offers structured methodologies for investigating alternative future scenarios, identifying potential intervention opportunities, and developing comprehensive strategies for intricate strategic environments.

Robustness and Sensitivity Testing

Strategic analysis gains practical value when it identifies robust insights that endure across variations in game parameters and assumptions. Robust testing systematically investigates how outcomes depend on specific modeling choices.

Parameter Sensitivity Analysis systematically explores how varying numerical parameters influence outcomes by testing payoff magnitude and ratio variations, probability distribution parameter changes, discount factor adjustments, or risk aversion coefficient modifications. This analysis elucidates which parameters critically determine results versus those where precise calibration is less critical.

Solution Concept Comparison investigates whether conclusions are contingent upon specific equilibrium definitions by comparing Nash, Perfect Bayesian, and Proper equilibrium predictions, contrasting evolutionary stability with strategic equilibrium, examining equilibrium selection criteria sensitivities, or comparing rationality-based versus learning-based predictions. This comparison identifies results that remain valid across solution concepts versus those that depend on specific rationality assumptions.

Bounded Rationality Exploration assesses the impact of limited cognitive capabilities on outcomes by employing constrained lookahead in sequential decisions. It models noisy best-response behaviors, incorporates cognitive hierarchy models (level-k thinking), or simulates satisficing rather than optimizing behaviors. This exploration elucidates which strategic insights remain valid when the assumption of perfect rationality is relaxed to more psychologically realistic models.

Initial Condition Sensitivity investigates how starting points influence evolutionary trajectories by varying initial strategy distributions, modifying initial belief structures, altering starting resource allocations, or changing initial network structures. This analysis distinguishes between path-dependent outcomes that critically depend on initial conditions versus robust attractors that emerge regardless of starting points.

Through a systematic analysis of result sensitivity, researchers can discern which strategic insights offer reliable guidance for practical applications, distinguishing robust conclusions from artifacts of specific modeling choices.

Modeling Conflicts and Collaborative Opportunities

Game theory provides specialized tools for analyzing two fundamental types of strategic situations that frequently arise in complex systems: conflicts, where participants have opposing interests, and coordination problems, where mutual benefit requires aligned actions. Understanding these situations helps identify both sources of system instability and opportunities for enhanced collaboration.

Conflict Analysis Frameworks

Several game-theoretic frameworks specifically address conflict situations where participants have partially or completely opposed interests.

Zero-Sum Analysis examines strictly competitive situations where one participant's gain precisely equals others' losses. This encompasses security strategies that maximize the minimum guaranteed outcomes, minimax/maximin solution concepts that address the worst-case optimization, mixed strategy optimization for situations requiring unpredictability, and value of information calculations in competitive intelligence contexts. These approaches elucidate fundamental conflicts where compromise is inconceivable, and strategic thinking must prioritize securing the optimal outcome against optimal opponent play.

Brinkmanship Models analyze conflicts involving escalation risks, where participants test resolution boundaries. These include crisis bargaining frameworks with incomplete information, escalation ladder structures with increasing cost/risk levels, reputation effects across repeated confrontations, and last-mover advantage dynamics in threat sequences. These models assist in understanding perilous conflict scenarios where participants deliberately create or accept risks to fortify their bargaining positions.

Contest and Tournament Models analyze competitive resource allocation to secure prizes. These models encompass various scenarios, including all-pay auctions where participants invest resources regardless of the outcome, Tullock contests where success probability is proportional to relative investment, multi-stage elimination tournaments, and arms race dynamics characterized by the security dilemma. These frameworks elucidate conflicts where competition itself consumes resources, potentially resulting in adverse outcomes for all participants despite rational individual decisions.

War of Attrition Games model conflicts where victory is achieved through outlasting opponents. These games involve exit decision dynamics under ongoing costs, incomplete information about opponent resources or resolve, signaling and reputation effects, and intervention timing optimization. These models provide insights into protracted conflicts where strategic patience and resource depth determine outcomes, ranging from competitive corporate standoffs to political confrontations.

By employing suitable conflict analysis frameworks, researchers can discern the underlying strategic dynamics that contribute to system instability, anticipate probable conflict trajectories, and devise intervention strategies that may mitigate detrimental consequences.

Coordination and Cooperation Models

In contrast to conflict situations, many strategic interactions involve potential mutual benefits through successful coordination or cooperation. These game-theoretic approaches specifically address the opportunities below:

- **Coordination Game Analysis** investigates scenarios where participants derive benefits from aligning their actions. These encompass pure coordination games, where any aligned choice benefits all parties; battle of the sexes structures with distinct preferred coordination points; stag hunt scenarios where coordination facilitates higher value but riskier opportunities; and focal point theory, which elucidates coordination without the need for communication. These frameworks elucidate how systems attain alignment when multiple equilibria coexist, and coordination benefits all parties.

- **Assurance Game Structures** model scenarios where mutual cooperation yields optimal outcomes but necessitates trust in the cooperation of others. These structures encompass trust development dynamics across repeated interactions, reputation mechanisms that support cooperative expectations, commitment devices that demonstrate cooperative intent, and verification systems that mitigate exploitation risks. These models elucidate how cooperative possibilities are contingent upon establishing adequate assurance against defection or exploitation.

- **Coalition Formation Analysis** investigates the formation of cooperative units within larger systems.

This encompasses core solutions that identify stable coalition structures, Shapley value and other equitable division concepts, mechanisms to prevent coalition dynamics that hinder exploitation, and coalition formation processes governed by diverse institutional rules. These approaches elucidate the likelihood and stability of collaborative arrangements within intricate multi-agent systems.

- **Mechanism Design for Cooperation** systematically develops structures that enable cooperation even when individual incentives conflict. These include binding agreement frameworks that enforce commitments, incentive-compatible arrangements that make honesty optimal, verification and monitoring systems that detect defection, and graduated sanction protocols that enforce cooperative norms. These approaches transcend analyzing existing games to design novel structures that facilitate cooperation when natural incentives prove inadequate.

By employing these frameworks, researchers can identify previously overlooked cooperative opportunities within intricate systems, design interventions that facilitate coordination, and establish institutional structures that sustain collaboration even in the face of individual temptations to defect.

Equilibrium Selection and Social Dynamics

In numerous strategic scenarios, the emergence of a specific outcome becomes paramount. This necessitates an understanding of equilibrium selection processes, which illuminate how systems navigate strategic ambiguity:

- **Focal Point Theory** elucidates the role of psychological salience in selecting among multiple equilibriums. It encompasses Schelling's notion of psychologically prominent solutions, cultural or contextual factors that foster shared expectations, labeling effects that establish coordination references, and precedent establishment through historical patterns. These concepts elucidate how systems resolve coordination challenges through shared psychological reference points rather than solely relying on strategic calculations.

- **Social Norm Evolution (SNE)** elucidates the emergence and persistence of behavioral standards through the process of norm emergence from repeated interactions. It posits the existence of sanctioning mechanisms that enforce compliance and meta-norms that mandate the participation of all individuals in enforcing norms. Additionally, SNE incorporates the dynamics of pluralistic ignorance and preference falsification, which can influence strategic choices beyond immediate payoff considerations. These frameworks provide insights into how social expectations shape strategic decisions, potentially stabilizing specific equilibrium.

- **Status and Hierarchy Effects** investigate the influence of social positioning on strategic behavior through prestige dynamics, deference patterns in sequential decision contexts, status competition motivating irrational choices, and authority structures that facilitate specific equilibria. These approaches recognize that social position considerations may drive strategic choices beyond mere material payoff maximization.

- **Narrative and Framing Influences** analyze how shared interpretations affect strategic decisions through problem framing effects on risk perception and decision-making, narrative structures that make certain strategies more compelling, identity considerations that constrain strategic options, and moral framing that activates non-material preferences. These perspectives acknowledge that meaning construction shapes strategic behavior, potentially determining which of multiple equilibria participants coordinate upon.

By comprehending these selection processes, we gain insights into why specific strategic outcomes manifest from the diverse possibilities that game theory frequently identifies. This comprehension proves particularly valuable in designing interventions that potentially redirect systems toward more desirable equilibria.

Case Study: Resource Competition in Limited Environments

To illustrate the practical application of game-theoretic approaches to complex systems, consider a case study involving resource competition among multiple stakeholder groups within a constrained environmental system. This case study demonstrates how game formulation, equilibrium analysis, and mechanism design can illuminate strategic dynamics and identify potential interventions.

This case concerns a regional watershed that supports diverse uses, including agricultural irrigation, municipal water supply, industrial production, and ecosystem maintenance. Historically, these uses had been managed under conditions of relative water abundance. However, climate change projections indicate substantial water supply reductions in the coming decades, potentially leading to destructive competition among stakeholders with varying priorities, time horizons, and political influence.

Key stakeholders in this case include the Agricultural Producers' Association, which represents farmers with historical water rights; the Municipal Water Authority, responsible for urban drinking water supply; the Industrial Consortium, which comprises manufacturing facilities requiring process water; the Environmental Protection Coalition, which advocates for ecosystem water allocations; the Hydropower Generator, which operates dams within the watershed; and the Regional Planning Commission, which possesses regulatory authority.

Traditional approaches to water allocation conflicts typically involved either litigation (resulting in winner-take-all outcomes) or regulatory mandates (often failing to account for stakeholder adaptations). Game theory provided an alternative analytical framework for understanding strategic incentives and designing more sustainable allocation mechanisms.

The strategic situation was conceptualized as a multifaceted game comprising various components.

Players were defined as the six stakeholder groups, each modeled as a unified actor with consistent preferences despite internal heterogeneity. This simplification struck a balance between analytical tractability and a realistic portrayal of the strategic environment.

Strategy spaces for each player encompassed decisions related to water extraction, including timing, volume, and location. Infrastructure investment choices included efficiency enhancements and storage capacity. Political action options encompassed lobbying, litigation, and coalition formation. Long-term adaptation strategies included crop selection and technology adoption. These multi-dimensional strategy spaces were parameterized to facilitate manageable representation while capturing the essential strategic options.

Payoff structures were modeled using economic value functions for various water uses, damage functions for water shortage impacts, cost functions for infrastructure investments, risk assessment models for climate variability, and discount factors reflecting different time preferences. These were calibrated using historical data, stakeholder interviews, and economic modeling to establish realistic representations of incentive structures.

Information structures incorporated uncertainty regarding future water availability, information asymmetry regarding actual water usage, incomplete knowledge of others' adaptation capabilities, and signaling opportunities through public commitments.

The overall formulation integrates elements of a repeated resource allocation game, a political influence contest, and a sequential investment game, reflecting the multifaceted nature of water management conflicts.

Equilibrium Analysis Results

Game-theoretic analysis revealed several important strategic dynamics:

- **Nash Equilibrium Analysis** identified a dominant competitive equilibrium characterized by accelerated water extraction to establish usage precedents, minimal investment in efficiency improvements, aggressive litigation to defend existing rights, and limited information sharing among stakeholders. This equilibrium represented a classic "tragedy of the commons" outcome, where individually rational strategies collectively produced suboptimal results for all participants.

- **Pareto Efficiency Assessment** revealed substantial disparities between the competitive equilibrium and attainable outcomes: total economic value approximately 40% below optimal allocation, unnecessary infrastructure duplication incurring approximately $120 million in costs, ecosystem damage resulting in approximately $80 million in unaccounted externalities, and litigation expenses consuming approximately $15 million annually. These efficiency gaps indicated substantial potential gains from alternative arrangements that could more effectively align individual incentives with collective outcomes.

- **Evolutionary Stability Analysis** investigated probable dynamics under limited rationality, revealing tit-for-tat extraction strategies as the dominant initial evolutionary strategy. Subsequently, retaliatory cycles generated escalating volatility. Leadership by dominant stakeholders catalyzed behavioral cascades. Learning processes converged toward competitive equilibrium. This analysis indicated that unmanaged strategic evolution would likely result in progressively destructive competition rather than spontaneously generating cooperative solutions.

Mechanism Design Application

Based on the game-theoretic analysis, a structured mechanism design process identified potential interventions that could alter strategic dynamics toward more productive equilibria.

Water Market Creation is a structured mechanism design process identified potential interventions that could shift strategic dynamics toward more productive equilibria. This market mechanism, designed with specific features such as clearly defined, tradable water rights with varying security levels, price discovery mechanisms accommodating seasonal variations, circuit-breaker provisions preventing extreme price volatility, and banking provisions enabling intertemporal transfers, addressed allocation efficiency while respecting existing rights distributions.

Risk-Pooling Institutions manage uncertainty through shared reservoir capacity with formulaic allocation rules, insurance mechanisms for shortage events, collective investment in prediction capabilities, and graduated response protocols for drought conditions. These institutions transformed zero-sum competition under uncertainty into shared risk management, creating mutual benefit opportunities.

Information-Sharing Systems with Strategic Design allow:

- Anonymous aggregate reporting protects competitive concerns.
- Third-party verification to maintain credibility.
- Advance commitment mechanisms to prevent opportunistic usage.
- Graduated transparency requirements scaled with shortage severity.

These systems overcame information asymmetries that hindered efficient coordination while safeguarding legitimate confidentiality concerns.

Long-Term Incentive Structures are:

- Infrastructure investment matching programs.
- Efficiency improvement tax incentives.
- Ecosystem service payment systems.
- Long-term contract frameworks with adjustment provisions.

These structures addressed temporal misalignment between immediate extraction incentives and long-term sustainability requirements.

Implementation and Outcomes

The game-theoretic analysis informed a two-year stakeholder negotiation process resulting in a comprehensive watershed management agreement incorporating many of the identified mechanism elements. Key implementation outcomes include strategic behavior changes observed among participants, including shifts from extraction maximization to optimization across time periods, increased investment in efficiency technologies, reduction in litigation in favor of mediated dispute resolution, and greater information sharing within structured frameworks.

Measurable performance improvements documented over the initial three years included a 23% reduction in total water usage while maintaining economic output, a 68% decrease in litigation expenses, a 47% increase in collaborative infrastructure investment, and stabilization of key ecosystem indicators.

Unexpected adaptive developments that emerged through implementation included the formation of sub-basin management consortia for localized solutions, development of water quality trading adjacent to quantity markets, creation of technical standards organizations for measurement systems, and evolution of informal reputation mechanisms that complemented formal structures.

The case demonstrates how game-theoretic analysis provided insights that were impossible to obtain through traditional approaches by explicitly modeling strategic interdependence, identifying efficiency-stability tensions, and designing mechanisms that transformed destructive competition into productive coordination.

Rather than imposing solutions through authority, the approach succeeded by realigning incentives to make cooperation strategically advantageous for all participants.

Conclusion

Game theory offers crucial analytical tools for comprehending strategic interactions within intricate systems. Game-theoretic models elucidate fundamental dynamics governing cooperation, conflict, and coordination by formalizing the interdependence among decision-makers, where optimal choices are contingent upon others' actions. These insights complement the behavioral fingerprinting and agent-based modeling approaches elucidated in previous chapters, augmenting our analytical framework with strategic depth.

The game formulation process constructs structured representations of strategic scenarios by identifying participants, defining strategy domains, modeling payoff structures, and specifying information conditions. These formulations facilitate equilibrium analysis through concepts such as Nash equilibrium, Pareto optimality, and evolutionary stability, enabling the prediction of probable outcomes and identifying potential intervention points. Simulation and scenario analysis extend beyond analytical solutions to explore evolutionary trajectories, examine counterfactual scenarios, and assess the robustness of results across diverse assumptions.

Game theory proves particularly valuable for comprehending two fundamental dynamics within complex systems: conflict situations involving opposing interests and coordination opportunities requiring aligned actions. Specialized frameworks for analyzing these situations aid in identifying both sources of system instability and possibilities for enhanced collaboration, thereby informing intervention design and mechanism development.

As exemplified in the watershed management case study, game-theoretic analysis can transform seemingly intractable conflicts into manageable strategic interactions by explicitly defining incentive structures, identifying efficiency-stability tensions, and designing mechanisms that align individual motivations with collective goals. Rather than imposing solutions through authority, this approach succeeds by creating conditions where cooperation becomes strategically advantageous for all participants.

The subsequent chapter will delve into network analysis techniques, illuminating communication and interaction pathways between system components. These methods complement game-theoretic understanding by revealing relationship structures that enable or constrain strategic interactions, providing another crucial dimension for comprehending complex systems of independent actors.

CHAPTER 7

Network Analysis for Communication Pathways

In previous chapters, we explored behavioral fingerprinting, agent-based modeling, and game-theoretic approaches. Now, we turn to another essential dimension of complex systems: the network structures that connect system components and shape information, resources, and influence flows. Network analysis provides powerful methods for understanding these relational patterns, revealing how system architecture enables or constrains interactions between independent actors.

While earlier chapters focused primarily on actor behaviors and strategic dynamics, network analysis focuses on the connections between actors, the channels through which information travels, resources flow, and influence spreads. These connection patterns often prove as important as individual characteristics in determining system outcomes.

> *A brilliant strategy without communication channels to spread it, a powerful actor isolated from resource flows, or an innovative idea disconnected from implementation pathways may all fail to influence system dynamics due to network constraints.*

This chapter delves into applying network analysis techniques to elucidate communication and interaction pathways within intricate systems. We explore methodologies for visualizing relationship structures, identifying influential positions, comprehending information dissemination dynamics, and analyzing the temporal evolution of networks. Throughout, we emphasize the integration of network insights with the comprehensive methodological framework established in preceding chapters, fostering a more nuanced understanding of complex multi-agent systems.

The initial step in network analysis entails creating visual representations that transform abstract relationship data into comprehensible maps of system connectivity. These visualizations unveil patterns imperceptible in tabular data, facilitating both exploratory investigation and compelling communication of network insights.

Network Representation Fundamentals

Networks, also known as graphs in mathematical terminology, comprise nodes (vertices) representing system entities and edges (links) representing relationships. This fundamental structure offers remarkable flexibility in representing diverse systems.

Node types vary depending on the system being studied. They can include individual actors (persons, organizations, autonomous agents), subgroups or communities within the system, resources or assets shared in environments, concepts, ideas, or information units, geographic locations or regions, and events or time periods.

Edge types correspond to various relationship dimensions, such as communication or information exchange, resource transfers or transactions, social relationships (friendship, trust, authority), influence or control pathways, physical connections or proximity, and similarity or association strength.

Network properties encompass various aspects, including directionality (edges can be directed or undirected), weighting (edges may carry weights indicating the strength, importance, or frequency of the relationship), multiplexity (multiple edge types can connect the same nodes), temporality (connections can form, strengthen, weaken, or dissolve over time), and attributes (both nodes and edges may possess additional attributes beyond basic connection data).

Effective network visualization necessitates deliberate decisions regarding how to represent these properties visually. Color, size, shape, and position can effectively encode network characteristics, while interactive features facilitate exploration across diverse scales and perspectives.

Layout Algorithms and Visualization Approaches

Transforming network data into comprehensible visualizations necessitates algorithms that strategically position nodes and edges to elucidate structural patterns. Several methodologies address this challenge:

- **Force-directed layouts** simulate physical interactions between nodes. Repulsive forces induce nodes to disperse to avoid collisions, while attractive forces draw connected nodes in proximity. The system iteratively refines until it achieves equilibrium. These layouts naturally cluster densely connected nodes, exposing communities and structural features without prior positioning. Algorithms such as Fruchterman-Reingold, ForceAtlas2, and D3-force generate intuitive visualizations where proximity accurately reflects connectivity.

- **Dimension reduction approaches** employ mathematical techniques to position nodes in two or three dimensions while preserving the network's structural integrity. Multidimensional scaling places similar nodes in proximity to one another, principal component analysis identifies the major structural dimensions, and t-SNE and UMAP preserve local neighborhood structures. These methods frequently yield more discernible visualizations for extensive networks, as force-directed layouts can become congested or computationally burdensome.

- **Circular and arc layouts** organize nodes around circles, with edges depicted as arcs. Nodes can be categorized or grouped into communities, and edge bundling minimizes visual clutter. Chord diagrams illustrate aggregate flows between groups. While these approaches prioritize visual clarity over structural clarity, they are particularly effective in highlighting group-level connections.

- **Hierarchical layouts** emphasize directional flows or organizational structures. Nodes are arranged in levels that indicate flow direction, tree layouts reveal branching structures, and radial hierarchies combine circular and hierarchical approaches. These visualizations excel at demonstrating authority relationships, information cascades, or organizational reporting structures.

- **Geospatial network visualization** integrates network data with geographic positioning. Nodes are positioned according to physical locations, edges indicate connections across geography, and map layers provide contextual information. These approaches are crucial for systems where physical geography significantly influences relationship patterns.

The selection of a layout algorithm should align with analytical objectives and network characteristics. Exploratory analysis may necessitate multiple visualization approaches to reveal diverse structural aspects, while communication-focused visualizations should prioritize the patterns most pertinent to the audience.

Multi-Level Visualization Strategies

Complex systems frequently possess multiple organizational levels, ranging from individual actors to subgroups and system-wide structures. Multi-level visualization strategies address this complexity by employing approaches that represent networks across diverse scales:

- **Hierarchical aggregation** visualizes networks at various granularity levels: micro-level depicting individual actor connections, meso-level aggregating actors into meaningful subgroups, and macro-level showcasing relationships between significant system components. Interactive implementations facilitate seamless zooming between levels, preserving context while unveiling pertinent details at each scale.

- **Nested network visualization** employs containment to represent multi-level structures. Higher-level entities are depicted as containers, encapsulating lower-level networks. Connections spanning levels are visually represented by crossing container boundaries. This

approach explicitly visualizes hierarchical organization
while maintaining the visibility of cross-level
relationships.

- **Multiple coordinated views** provide diverse perspectives
  on the same network: overview visualizations
  showcasing the entire network structure, detail views
  focusing on specific subnetworks, alternative
  representations highlighting different relationship
  dimensions, and supplementary visualizations displaying
  node or edge attributes. Coordinated selection and
  filtering across views facilitate exploration of how
  patterns at one scale or dimension relate to others.

- **Temporal sequence visualization** demonstrates network
  evolution over time through animation, which illustrates
  dynamic structural changes. Small multiple displays
  showcase network states at various points in time, while
  timeline interfaces enable temporal navigation. Change
  highlighting emphasizes emerging or dissolving
  structures. These approaches reveal network evolution,
  potentially revealing pattern formation, structural
  dissolution, or cyclic changes that are inaccessible in
  static representations.

- **Multi-level visualization** strategies transform the
  overwhelming complexity of networks into
  comprehensible visual narratives, enabling analysts to

navigate across scales and dimensions while maintaining a coherent understanding of system structure.

Identifying Key Influencers

Beyond visual representation, network analysis offers quantitative methods for identifying strategically significant positions within relationship structures. These methods assist in pinpointing actors who disproportionately influence information flow, resource distribution, or system behavior through their network positioning.

Centrality Measures

Centrality metrics quantify various aspects of positional importance within networks, each capturing distinct dimensions of influence potential.

Degree centrality measures an actor's number of direct connections. In undirected networks, it refers to the number of connections to other nodes. In directed networks, both in-degree (incoming connections) and out-degree (outgoing connections) are considered. In weighted networks, it calculates the sum of connection weights. High degree centrality indicates actors with numerous direct relationships, potentially enabling information access, resource gathering, or direct influence over many others. However, this measure focuses solely on immediate connections without considering the broader network structure.

Betweenness centrality assesses an actor's positioning along paths connecting other nodes. It calculates the shortest paths between all node pairs, determines the number of shortest paths passing through each node, and normalizes by the total number of paths. High betweenness centrality identifies actors who frequently serve as bridges or gatekeepers, controlling information or resource flow between otherwise disconnected system segments. These positions often enable coordination, integration, or strategic information control even without numerous direct connections.

Closeness centrality measures an actor's average distance to all other nodes by calculating the shortest path length to every other node and taking the reciprocal of the average path length. High closeness centrality indicates actors who can efficiently reach or be reached by many others through relatively short paths. These positions enable rapid information dissemination, comprehensive situation awareness, or system-wide influence through relatively few intermediate steps.

Eigenvector centrality[17] measures connection to other central nodes by iteratively calculating centrality based on neighbors' centrality and stabilizing through eigenvector computation of the adjacency matrix. High eigenvector centrality identifies actors connected to other well-connected actors, capturing the recursive nature of influence where connections to influential nodes

---

[17] Eigenvector centrality is a sophisticated measure of influence in network analysis that evaluates a node's importance based not just on how many connections it has, but on the quality of those connections.

provide greater influence than connections to peripheral ones. This measure particularly suits status or prestige dynamics, where importance is derived from association with other important actors.

PageRank[18] adapts eigenvector centrality for directed networks. It incorporates directed connection patterns, includes a dampening factor modeling random jumps, and converges to stable rank values through iteration. Initially developed for web page ranking, PageRank effectively measures potential attention or information flow in systems where directed connections (like citations, recommendations, or authority relationships) determine influence patterns.

Katz centrality extends eigenvector centrality by incorporating path attenuation. It calculates the centrality of each node by considering all walks between nodes with distance-based discounting. An adjustable attenuation factor controls the influence decay with distance, ensuring that the measure converges even in networks where eigenvector centrality fails. This measure effectively captures influence propagating through networks with diminishing strength over longer paths, providing a more accurate representation of various real-world influence mechanisms.

---

[18] PageRank fundamentally transformed how search engines evaluate the importance of web pages by applying network analysis principles to the structure of the web.

Each centrality measure reveals different aspects of positional importance. Comprehensive analysis typically employs multiple measures to identify influential actors in different ways, from direct connection hubs to critical bridges to prestigious central figures.

Community Detection and Structural Roles

Beyond individual positional significance, network analysis elucidates how actors cluster into communities and assume distinctive structural roles that influence system dynamics:

- **Community detection algorithms** identify densely connected subgroups through modularity optimization (identifying divisions maximizing internal connections relative to expected random connections), hierarchical clustering (constructing nested community structures through divisive or agglomerative processes), label propagation (assigning communities through iterative majority-rule voting among neighbors), and statistical inference (fitting generative models of community structure to observed network data). These algorithms unveil natural groupings that may correspond to functional teams, ideological factions, geographical regions, or other meaningful subcommunities within the broader system.

- **Core-periphery analysis** distinguishes central cores from peripheral regions by identifying densely connected core nodes from sparsely connected peripheries. Coreness is measured through k-core decomposition or continuous core scores. This analysis identifies multiple cores in polycentric networks and tracks core stability and periphery mobility over time. This analysis reveals a hierarchical organization, where core members maintain dense interconnections while peripheral members connect primarily to the core rather than each other.

- **Structural equivalence** identifies nodes with comparable connection patterns by computing similarity in connection profiles across nodes, clustering nodes based on connection pattern similarity, and identifying substitutable positions within network structures. This approach unveils role-based organization, wherein distinct actors occupy equivalent positions without necessarily establishing direct connections.

Brokerage Role Analysis: Unraveling Community Connections

Brokerage role analysis elucidates the functions of nodes that facilitate communication between communities. Coordinators connect members within their own communities, gatekeepers control access to their communities from external sources, representatives manage outward connections from their communities, consultants connect diverse communities without belonging to any, and liaisons bridge between multiple communities without membership in any. These roles highlight critical functions in managing cross-boundary relationships, often demonstrating greater significance than simple centrality measures in comprehending system integration and information flow.

By identifying communities and structural roles, network analysis unveils organizational principles beyond individual connections, illuminating how system architecture fosters functional differentiation and integration across subcomponents.

Influence Pathway Mapping

Understanding the propagation of influence through networks necessitates identifying specific pathways through which information, resources, or behavioral changes traverse from their origins to their destinations.

Path analysis determines specific connection sequences through the shortest paths (minimum number of steps between nodes). All-paths analysis enumerates all routes between nodes. K-step paths identify connections requiring exactly k intermediaries. Maximum flow analysis aggregates capacity across all possible paths. These analyses reveal specific routes through which influence travels, identifying critical junctions, alternative pathways, and potential bottlenecks.

Diffusion modeling simulates the dissemination of information or influence through various threshold models, such as nodes adopting a state when a sufficient number of neighboring nodes have already done so. It also incorporates independent cascade models, where each activation generates independent activation probabilities. Additionally, it encompasses SI/SIR/SIS models, which are epidemiological frameworks applied to the spread of information. Furthermore, Bass diffusion combines external influences with network-based adoption. These models predict the information or behavior propagation rate and the likelihood of different network regions receiving information early, late, or potentially not at all.

Flow decomposition systematically breaks down aggregate relationships into constituent pathways by quantifying the contributions of source-target pairs to the overall flow. It decomposes flows into elementary paths, assesses path diversity and redundancy, and identifies critical paths that carry disproportionate flow. This analysis elucidates which specific routes most significantly contribute to overall system connectivity, enabling the prioritization of relationships that warrant the closest attention or protection.

Causal pathway analysis elucidates the propagation of effects through network structures by tracing influence chains through mediation analysis. It identifies indirect effects via multi-step pathways, quantifies path-specific contributions to overall effects, and controls for confounding relationships in causal inference. This approach distinguishes direct influence from indirect effects mediated through network pathways, providing a more accurate understanding of causal mechanisms in interconnected systems.

Influence pathway mapping transforms static network representations into dynamic insights into how positioning facilitates or impedes propagation processes. It elucidates why certain positions exert disproportionate influence despite potentially modest direct connectivity.

CHAPTER 8

Information Dissemination
and Temporal Network Analysis

I nformation flow represents one of the most critical processes
shaped by network structures. Understanding how network
architecture affects information dissemination patterns helps
explain knowledge distribution, opinion formation, and
coordination capabilities within complex systems.

Information Flow Dynamics

Several fundamental dynamics govern the dissemination of
information through networks, resulting in characteristic patterns
that significantly impact system behavior.

Transmission mechanisms dictate how information is transferred
between interconnected entities. Push mechanisms involve

actively distributing information from senders to recipients, while pull mechanisms involve recipients actively seeking information from sources. Subscription models enable recipients to receive automatic updates from selected sources. Broadcast patterns disseminate information simultaneously to multiple recipients, while narrowcast patterns target specific recipients based on attributes or relationships. These mechanisms generate distinct flow patterns, with push systems typically resulting in broader but shallower distribution than pull systems, which generate narrower but often deeper engagement.

Filtering processes determine which information is transmitted through specific network pathways. Attention allocation constraints limit cognitive capacity and restrict information processing. Relevance filtering enables actors to prioritize information that aligns with their interests or needs. Trust-based filtering determines the credibility of the source and the acceptance of information. Confirmation bias leads actors to preferentially transmit information that confirms their existing beliefs. Novelty filtering gives priority attention to unusual or surprising information. These filtering processes demonstrate that network connectivity alone does not guarantee information transfer; content characteristics and relationship qualities significantly influence the actual propagation of information.

Transformation patterns elucidate the alterations that transpire during the transmission of information. Compression condenses intricate information into succinct summaries or pivotal points. Elaboration expands fundamental information by incorporating interpretations or contextual details. Recombination merges elements from disparate information sources into novel forms. Distortion modifies information through misinterpretations or reframings. Validation or invalidation fortifies or diminishes information through verification processes. These transformations result in substantial variations in the information reaching remote network regions, potentially leading to misalignments between the sources and destinations of the information.

Temporal dynamics govern the propagation and persistence of information within a network. Propagation speed quantifies the rate at which information traverses different regions, while decay patterns elucidate the gradual diminution of information relevance or accuracy over time. Refresh cycles indicate the frequency with which information updates replace previous versions, and persistence variations reveal the duration of information's active presence in various network areas. These temporal characteristics establish asynchronous information environments, where distinct network regions operate with varying information versions and update schedules.

Understanding these dynamics helps explain why seemingly simple information distribution processes often produce complex patterns of knowledge diversity, opinion clustering, and coordination challenges within networked systems.

Network Structures and Information Access

Different network architectures generate distinctive information distribution patterns, significantly impacting the access of information by various entities. Several structural features particularly influence information access:

- **Centralization versus decentralization** determines information aggregation patterns. Centralized networks effectively collect information but create bottlenecks and single failure points. Decentralized networks provide redundant pathways but may fragment information across disconnected regions. Hybrid structures with multiple hubs often strike a balance between efficiency and resilience. The degree of centralization significantly affects the extent to which any single actor can access system-wide information, with implications for coordination capabilities and vulnerability to targeted disruptions.

- **Clustering and community structures** establish information distribution boundaries. Information circulates swiftly within densely interconnected clusters, while cross-cluster transmission occurs more gradually and selectively. Strong clustering generates information silos with distinct knowledge bases, while cross-cutting ties that bridge clusters expedite system-wide dissemination. These structures elucidate why information frequently remains confined within subcommunities despite theoretical connectivity to broader networks, resulting in knowledge or belief differentiation between network regions.

- **Small-world properties** significantly influence system-wide information access. Most real-world networks exhibit both high clustering and short average path lengths. These structures enable information to spread widely while maintaining local coherence. Strategic "weak ties" connecting otherwise distant regions facilitate rapid system-wide dissemination, while removing key bridging connections can dramatically increase information diffusion time. The presence or absence of small-world properties fundamentally determines how rapidly and completely information can permeate entire networks, with significant implications for coordination capability and adaptation speed.

- **Core-periphery organizations** generate asymmetric information environments. Core members gain access to information from multiple sources with cross-validation opportunities, while peripheral members primarily receive filtered information through limited core connections. Information originating from the periphery must undergo gatekeeping by core members to achieve widespread dissemination. Core positions provide information advantages that often translate into decision influence. These structures establish predictable information asymmetries that shape power dynamics, with core positioning conferring substantial informational advantages beyond mere connection volume.

- **Hierarchical structures** establish distinct vertical information flows. Upward flows accumulate information from dispersed sources, while downward flows distribute directives or processed intelligence. Informal information pathways are created through skip-level connections that bypass intermediate layers, and information transformation typically occurs at each hierarchical level. These patterns elucidate why organizations frequently encounter challenges in accurate information transfer across hierarchical levels, with practical implications for organizational design and communication strategies.

Understanding the functional role of these structural features in shaping information access elucidates the mechanisms underlying knowledge diversity, belief clustering, and coordination difficulties in intricate systems, despite nominal connectivity among components.

Information bottlenecks, which arise from network structures that restrict information flow, significantly impact system performance by hindering coordination, learning, and adaptation capabilities. Network analysis offers several methods for identifying and addressing these constraints:

- **Structural hole analysis** calculates network constraint measures to identify missing connections that fragment information flow. It also identifies redundant connectivity and bridging opportunities between disconnected clusters, measures the efficiency of existing bridges in transferring specific information types, and analyzes strategic advantages available to actors spanning structural holes. This analysis reveals potential areas where targeted connection creation could substantially enhance information distribution efficiency.

- **Minimum cut identification** is a technique used to identify vulnerable connection sets within a network. It achieves this by determining the minimum set of connections that, if removed, would sever network regions. Additionally, it calculates the maximum flow capacity between critical node pairs, locates "narrow waist" connections that carry disproportionate information volume, and assesses connectivity redundancy between significant network regions. These analyses reveal vulnerable connection points where disruption would severely affect system-wide information flow.

- **Transmission delay mapping** identifies slow information pathways by measuring actual information propagation times between network regions. It compares empirical transmission speeds with theoretical minimums, identifying high-delay connections that create effective information barriers. Additionally, it locates queuing points where information backlogs develop. This approach focuses on actual transmission performance rather than just structural connectivity, accounting for capacity constraints that structural analysis alone may overlook.

- **Information overload detection** identifies nodes struggling with processing capacity by measuring information volume flowing through high-centrality nodes. It compares processing demands with cognitive or technological capacity, identifying the severity of filtering required to manage incoming information, and analyzing distortion patterns resulting from overload management strategies. This analysis recognizes that even well-connected nodes may become functional bottlenecks when information volume exceeds processing capacity.

- **Cross-boundary translation** challenges identify the points of information transformation during transmission by locating interfaces between specialized communities. They also identify terminology or conceptual framework incompatibilities, measure interpretation variation across community boundaries, and analyze the effectiveness of boundary-spanning objects or individuals. This approach recognizes that connectivity alone does not guarantee understanding, especially when information crosses between communities with distinct knowledge bases or interpretive frameworks.

- **Network analysis** facilitates targeted interventions to enhance information flow by identifying specific bottleneck types and locations. This can involve creating new connections, increasing processing capacity, or improving cross-boundary translation mechanisms.

Temporal Network Analysis

Networks rarely remain static; they undergo evolution as relationships develop, strengthen, weaken, and dissolve. Temporal network analysis investigates these dynamic processes, elucidating how relationship structures transform over time and how these alterations impact system functionality.

Network evolution exhibits characteristic patterns influenced by both endogenous dynamics (originating from the network itself) and exogenous factors (originating from external influences). Several key evolutionary processes warrant specific attention.

Growth mechanisms determine the expansion of networks over time. Preferential attachment leads to new nodes connecting preferentially to already well-connected nodes. Triadic closure occurs when connections form between nodes sharing mutual connections. Homophily-driven growth involves the formation of connections between similar nodes. Geographic constraint influences connection formation probability based on physical proximity. Strategic attachment involves the formation of connections based on calculated advantages rather than structural position. These mechanisms generate distinctive growth signatures, ranging from scale-free structures arising from preferential attachment to clustered communities emerging from homophily and triadic closure.

The processes of decay and pruning determine the disappearance of connections in networks. Activity-based decay involves the gradual weakening and eventual disappearance of unused connections. Resource constraint pruning occurs when limited capacity necessitates selective connection maintenance. Strategic termination entails ending connections based on calculated disadvantages. External disruption, such as environmental changes, leads to the dissolution of connections. Cascade failures result from initial disconnections triggering further connection losses.

These processes collectively explain why networks rarely grow indefinitely but instead attain dynamic equilibria where the formation of new connections balances ongoing connection loss.

Rewiring dynamics elucidate the reorganization of connection patterns within networks. Optimization processes facilitate the shift of connections to maximize value or minimize costs. Exploration-exploitation balancing involves alternating between stable utilization and novel possibility testing. Adaptation to external changes necessitates reorganizing connection patterns to address evolving environmental conditions. Learning processes enable the adjustment of connection patterns based on performance feedback. These dynamics demonstrate how networks maintain functional continuity amidst ongoing structural change, with rewiring processes facilitating adaptation without complete reorganization.

Cyclical patterns manifest recurring structural transformations. Expansion-contraction cycles characterize networks as alternating between growth and consolidation phases. Centralization-decentralization oscillations involve the shift of control structures between concentrated and distributed arrangements. Specialization-integration phases entail networks cycling between functional differentiation and cross-functional integration. Formal-informal alternation entails the transition of relationship patterns between institutionalized and emergent structures. These cycles frequently reflect fundamental tensions within networked systems, oscillating between complementary organizing principles rather than permanent resolutions toward extremes.

Comprehending these evolutionary processes elucidates the reasons behind the persistence of certain network structures while others exhibit transience, offering insights into both current organization and potential future developments.

Analyzing network dynamics necessitates specialized metrics and methodologies that transcend static structural measures. Several approaches prove particularly valuable:

- **Temporal centrality** measures track positional significance over time. Time-aware betweenness measures account for positional differences in time-ordered paths. Temporal closeness captures reachability based on connection timing. Temporal eigenvector centrality influences accounting for connection sequences. Dynamic activity centrality identifies consistently active nodes across time periods. These measures elucidate how actor positioning evolves and identify consistently influential positions even amidst structural reorganization.

- **Stability and volatility** metrics quantify structural change rates. Edge persistence measures the duration of typical connections. Turnover rates quantify the percentage of connections that change over a time period. Jaccard similarity measures the overlap between network states at different time points. Rank stability tracks the persistence of centrality rankings over time. These metrics distinguish between relatively stable and highly volatile network regions, revealing where structure provides reliable constraints versus where relationships remain in flux.

- **Temporal motif** analysis elucidates characteristic temporal connection patterns. Recurrent interaction sequences identify frequently repeated connection chronologies. Burst patterns detect temporal clustering of connection activities. Causal sequence detection identifies reliable ordering in connection formation. Cycle identification discovers regularly recurring connection patterns. This analysis unveils distinctive micro-level temporal signatures that influence macro-level network evolution.

- **Change-point detection** identifies significant structural transitions. Community rearrangement detection identifies instances when group structures undergo substantial reorganization. Centralization shift identification detects transitions between various influence structures. Connectivity regime changes identify transformations in fundamental connection patterns. External shock response analysis quantifies how external events trigger structural reorganization. These methods emphasize critical transition periods when network structures undergo fundamental reorganization rather than merely incremental adjustment.

- **Predictive modeling** forecasts future structural developments. Link prediction estimates the likelihood of new connections forming. Community evolution prediction projects the development of group structures.

Influence shift forecasting predicts changes in positional importance. Stability assessment evaluates which structures are likely to persist versus transform. These approaches extend beyond descriptive analysis to anticipate upcoming changes, enabling a proactive response to emerging structural developments.

- **Temporal network analysis** transforms static structural understanding into dynamic process models, revealing how networks function as evolving systems rather than fixed architectures.

Resilience and Adaptation Assessment

Network structures significantly influence how systems respond to disruptions and changing conditions:

- **Temporal network analysis** provides methods for assessing resilience, the ability to maintain function despite disturbance—and adaptation capability, the ability to reorganize in response to changing requirements.

- **Structural vulnerability analysis** identifies how disruptions affect connectivity. Targeted attack simulation models connectivity loss when high-centrality nodes are removed. Random failure testing assesses robustness against random connection disruptions. Cascading failure modeling simulates how initial disruptions propagate through dependent connections. Recovery path analysis maps how connectivity is restored after disruption. These analyses reveal which network structures provide robust connectivity despite both targeted and random disruptions.

- **Functional resilience assessment** evaluates the impact of structural modifications on system performance. Critical function mapping identifies the network structures that facilitate essential system operations. Redundancy analysis quantifies alternative pathways for key processes. Graceful degradation testing assesses the gradual decline of performance rather than catastrophic failure. Minimum viable network identification determines the essential connections required for basic functionality. This assessment establishes the correlation between structural resilience and actual performance outcomes, acknowledging that topological connectivity alone does not guarantee functional continuity.

- **Adaptation mechanisms** elucidate how networks reorganize in response to change. Compensatory rewiring entails the formation of novel connections that compensate for lost functionality. Load redistribution involves redistributing functions from disrupted to intact network regions. Modular reconfiguration entails reorganizing component relationships while preserving module integrity. Scalability mechanisms are processes that maintain function despite substantial size alterations. These mechanisms elucidate how certain networks maintain functional continuity despite significant structural reorganization.

- **Early warning indicator analysis** identifies impending critical transitions. Increasing connection volatility indicates growing instability in relationship patterns. Critical slowing down implies that the system requires extended recovery periods from minor perturbations. Rising cross-scale correlation suggests synchronization across previously independent network regions. Flickering behavior indicates that the system momentarily exhibits alternative structural states. These indicators assist in identifying vulnerability periods when networks approach tipping points between distinct structural regimes.

- **Adaptation rate assessment** quantifies the speed at which networks reorganize in response to environmental changes. Structural lag measurement quantifies the time delay between environmental alterations and the subsequent reorganization of the network. Learning curve analysis determines the rate of improvement in structural alignment with novel conditions. The exploration-exploitation balance represents the trade-off between maintaining structural stability and engaging in adaptive searching. Path dependency effects demonstrate how historical structures constrain the adaptability of networks. This assessment enables determining whether networks possess the requisite adaptability to match the pace of environmental change.

By integrating these methodologies, analysts can simultaneously assess both current resilience and long-term adaptation potential. This analysis identifies the strengths of existing structures in providing robust performance and the potential for strategic reorganization to enhance adaptability.

Case Study: Information Flow in Social Networks

To illustrate the practical application of network analysis techniques, let us examine a case study involving the diffusion of information through social networks during crisis response. This case study demonstrates how visualization, centrality analysis, community detection, and temporal network methods can provide actionable insights for enhancing emergency communication effectiveness.

Context and Analytical Objectives

The case involved analyzing information dissemination patterns during a regional flooding emergency that affected multiple communities. Emergency management officials sought to understand why critical safety information reached some community segments rapidly while others received delayed, distorted, or no information despite broadcast distribution through official channels.

Initial assumptions focused on demographic factors or technology access as primary explanatory variables. However, network analysis revealed that social relationship structures fundamentally shaped information flow beyond these individual attributes, creating both unexpected transmission pathways and significant distribution barriers.

The analysis integrated data from multiple sources: social media interaction patterns before and during the emergency, mobile phone communication metadata (anonymized and aggregated), emergency service communication logs, post-event community surveys on information sources, and organizational network data from key community institutions. These diverse data sources enabled the construction of multiplex network models capturing different communication channels and relationship types that collectively shaped information dissemination.

Network Visualization Results

Visualization techniques transformed intricate relationship data into comprehensible maps of community communication structures:

- **Community cluster visualization** identified five distinct communication communities largely corresponding to geographic neighborhoods. Three communities were organized around shared languages (English, Spanish, and Vietnamese). Work-based communication clusters transcended residential communities. Faith community networks form cross-cutting connections. Additionally, there was significant variation in cross-cluster connectivity, with some communities exhibiting near-isolation.

- **Information source mapping** revealed that official emergency information primarily originated from sources with strong connections to English-speaking and higher-income communities. Informal information hubs emerged within each community cluster. Critical information was translated and contextualized by specific boundary-spanning individuals. Furthermore, visual confirmation confirmed substantial information access disparities across community segments.

- **Temporal flow visualization** revealed initial information concentration in official channels and directly connected communities, facilitating dissemination through high-centrality nodes within each community. Significant time delays were observed across certain community boundaries, while information transformation patterns emerged as content traversed between communities.

- **Multi-channel integration** demonstrated the complementary functions of various communication technologies: face-to-face communication remained indispensable for trust-based information exchange, social media facilitated rapid but often incomplete information distribution, text messaging facilitated the highest-trust transmission for close relationships, and radio and traditional media reached previously underserved population segments.

These visualizations transformed abstract data into tangible insights into how community structure influenced information access, unveiling previously inaccessible patterns in non-network analysis.

Key Influencer Analysis

Centrality measures identified individuals and organizations occupying strategically important network positions that disproportionately influenced information flow:

- **Betweenness centrality analysis** identified key boundary spanners connecting otherwise separated communities, cultural brokers translating information between language communities, organizations serving as cross-community information hubs, and critical bottlenecks where information flow depended on single connections.

- Eigenvector centrality assessment revealed official information sources with high formal authority but limited actual influence, informal community leaders with exceptional information distribution capability, variation in influential actors across different communication channels, and misalignment between formal emergency communication strategies and actual influence patterns.

- **Community-specific influence** mapping revealed distinct internal influence structures within each community. Specific individuals served as primary information access points for subgroups, trust relationships determined which sources received attention during uncertainty, and different influence mechanisms operated across socioeconomic boundaries.

- **Cross-channel influence integration** demonstrated that some individuals maintained high centrality across multiple communication platforms, while others exhibited channel-specific influence limited to particular technologies. Complementary influence patterns emerged where different actors controlled different dissemination mechanisms. Official sources typically dominated broadcast channels, while informal influencers controlled interpersonal channels.

This analysis transformed generic "community outreach" into targeted engagement with specific individuals occupying pivotal network positions, significantly enhancing information dissemination efficiency.

Community Structure Impact

Analysis of community structures unveiled how group organization generated both information distribution challenges and untapped dissemination opportunities:

- **Modularity analysis** quantified community boundaries, creating significant information transmission friction. Stronger boundaries were observed around language-based versus geography-based communities, certain institutional communities (schools, religious organizations) maintaining high internal cohesion, and variation in boundary permeability across different information types.

- **Bridge analysis** identified specific organizations serving as critical cross-community connectors. Individuals maintaining membership in multiple communities were also identified. Weak but crucial ties were found connecting otherwise separated populations. Additionally, institutional relationships were noted as creating formal bridges between communities.

- **Information silo mapping** revealed communities receiving abundant information that remained internally trapped. Feedback loops reinforced and amplified information within closed communities, leading to echo chamber effects that created community-specific interpretations of the same base information. Additionally, missing connections prevented information validation across sources.

- **Temporal community evolution** demonstrated that community boundaries temporarily strengthened during initial crisis phases, gradually becoming more permeable throughout the crisis timeline. New bridges were formed in response to information needs, while some communities experienced increased isolation as crisis response efforts appeared to exclude them.

This community-focused analysis elucidated why broadcast dissemination strategies often failed to achieve uniform coverage, underscoring the necessity for community-specific transmission strategies that leverage existing structures rather than attempting to override them.

Temporal Dynamics and Adaptation

Temporal network analysis elucidated the evolution of communication patterns during the crisis, uncovering both problematic disruptions and effective adaptive responses:

- **Information propagation tracking** monitored the dissemination of official safety information to high-socioeconomic communities within 30 minutes, while the same information required more than 3 hours to reach certain immigrant communities. Furthermore, critical information was never disseminated to approximately 15% of residents. Additionally, specific transmission pathways accounted for the majority of successful cross-community dissemination.

- **Adaptation pattern identification** revealed the spontaneous emergence of novel communication hubs during infrastructure disruptions. Power-affected areas experienced shifts from digital to face-to-face communication. As the crisis progressed, information flow became increasingly centralized. Informal validation mechanisms for rumor control emerged.

These insights led to significant improvements in emergency communication strategies. Network analysis transformed our understanding of information dissemination processes and guided more effective interventions in complex social systems.

Conclusion

Network analysis provides crucial tools for comprehending how relationship structures influence system behavior by either facilitating or inhibiting interaction, communication, and influence pathways. By unveiling connection patterns that are concealed in non-relational analysis, these methodologies assist in elucidating why seemingly identical interventions yield disparate outcomes in diverse contexts, why information dissemination occurs unevenly despite broadcast distribution, and how strategic positioning often holds greater significance than individual attributes in determining system-level influence.

The visualization techniques elucidated within this chapter transform abstract relationship data into intuitive maps that elucidate structural patterns and facilitate intervention design. Centrality measures and community detection methods identify strategically important positions and group structures that disproportionately shape system dynamics. Information flow analysis elucidates how network architecture generates characteristic distribution patterns that determine the dissemination of information, including the recipients, timeliness, and certainty. Temporal network methods reveal how these structures evolve over time, providing insights into both resilience against disruption and adaptability in evolving environments.

As illustrated in the crisis communication case study, these analytical approaches can yield actionable insights for improving system performance—from identifying influential individuals for targeted engagement to locating structural bottlenecks that necessitate bridging. Furthermore, they can elucidate community boundaries that influence information interpretation and trust. Rather than treating systems as independent entities, network analysis unveils the relational structures that fundamentally determine how components interact to yield system-level outcomes.

In the subsequent chapter, we will delve into how LLMs can augment our interpretation capabilities for intricate systems, augmenting our analytical framework with a potent tool. These models possess advanced natural language processing capabilities that harmonize with the structural understanding derived from network analysis, offering novel methodologies for extracting meaning from unorganized data and identifying conceptual patterns across diverse information sources.

Large Language Models for Interpretation

Having established methodologies for behavioral fingerprinting, agent-based modeling, game-theoretic analysis, and network mapping in previous chapters, we now turn to a powerful technology for interpreting the vast amounts of data generated by complex systems: LLMs. These sophisticated AI systems transform how analysts process, synthesize, and derive meaning from the complex patterns, interactions, and emergent behaviors characteristic of multi-agent systems.

> *The fundamental challenge in complex systems analysis lies not only in data collection or pattern identification, but also in comprehending and utilizing this information effectively.*

As systems become increasingly complex, encompassing a wider range of agents, interactions, behavioral dimensions, and temporal dynamics, the resulting data often exceeds human cognitive capacity. LLMs address this challenge by serving as cognitive partners that can process vast information volumes, identify patterns across diverse domains, generate coherent narratives that elucidate system behavior, and facilitate translation between specialized knowledge domains.

This chapter delves into the application of LLMs in enhancing complex systems analysis. It examines LLMs' capabilities for data summarization, pattern interpretation, hypothesis generation, and interdisciplinary knowledge integration. Practical implementation approaches, limitation management strategies, and validation techniques are discussed to ensure the reliability of insights derived from LLMs. The chapter culminates in integrating LLM capabilities with the analytical framework developed in previous chapters, establishing a comprehensive methodology for comprehending complex systems composed of independent actors.

Data Summarization Capabilities

The volume, variety, and velocity of data generated by intricate systems frequently surpass traditional analytical methodologies. LLMs provide potent summarization capabilities that transform overwhelming data volumes into comprehensible and actionable insights while ensuring the preservation of crucial information.

Multi-Source Synthesis

Complex systems analysis typically draws from diverse data sources, including quantitative metrics, network structures, behavioral observations, textual communications, and temporal patterns. LLMs excel at synthesizing these heterogeneous data types into coherent summaries:

- **Cross-modal integration** combines information across different data formats. LLMs can produce textual summaries of numerical patterns and statistical results, create narrative descriptions of network structures and their implications, develop integrated timelines connecting quantitative changes with qualitative events, and generate behavioral interpretations of interaction data and transaction records. This integration provides a holistic understanding that is impossible to achieve through siloed analysis of individual data streams, revealing how different system aspects interrelate.

- **Multi-level summarization** offers insights at appropriate granularity levels. LLMs can generate executive summaries capturing essential system dynamics in a concise format, detailed technical summaries preserving methodological nuance and analytical depth, domain-specific extracts focusing on specific system aspects, and comparative summaries highlighting similarities and differences across subsystems. This hierarchical approach ensures information accessibility for diverse stakeholders while maintaining a connection to the underlying analytical depth.

- **Contextual prioritization** focuses attention on situation-relevant information. LLMs can highlight anomalous patterns requiring immediate attention, emphasize findings addressing specific research questions, foreground actionable insights while contextualizing background information, and adapt emphasis based on audience expertise and decision responsibilities. This capability transforms generic data summaries into targeted information packages that support specific understanding needs and decision contexts.

- **Temporal compression** condenses extended timelines into comprehensible narratives. LLMs can identify pivotal events and turning points in system evolution, recognize imperceptible gradual patterns in short-term analysis, connect seemingly unrelated events into coherent causal sequences, and distinguish between cyclical patterns and directional trends. This temporal synthesis facilitates analysts' comprehension of system evolution spanning timeframes beyond direct observation, providing essential historical context and future trajectory insights.

By transforming voluminous data into structured and accessible summaries, LLMs empower human analysts to maintain comprehensive awareness of intricate system dynamics without cognitive strain. They effectively augment human information processing capacity while preserving human judgment and contextual understanding.

Extractive vs. Generative Summarization

LLMs employ two complementary summarization approaches, each with distinct advantages for complex systems analysis:

- **Extractive summarization** identifies and selects existing content representing key information. This entails selecting representative sentences or paragraphs from source documents, highlighting critical data points from larger datasets, identifying exemplary cases that illustrate broader patterns, and extracting pivotal moments from extended interaction sequences. This approach directly connects to the original data, providing transparent traceability between summaries and sources. When precise wording and specific details are of paramount importance, extractive methods preserve the original formulations while reducing the volume.

- **Generative summarization** generates novel content that encapsulates the core essence of the input. This encompasses integrating multiple sources into cohesive narratives, translating technical data into comprehensible language, developing conceptual abstractions that elucidate underlying patterns, and constructing explanatory frameworks that establish connections between disparate observations. This methodology excels at identifying higher-order patterns and implications not explicitly stated in the source materials. When the integration and interpretation of information are of paramount importance over a verbatim reproduction, generative methods provide a superior level of insight value.

- **Hybrid approaches** combine both methods to achieve optimal results. This includes using extraction for precise factual information requiring accuracy, applying generation for integration, interpretation, and implication development, maintaining a clear distinction between direct quotations and synthetic conclusions, and providing explicit traceability between generated insights and supporting evidence. These hybrid techniques leverage the complementary strengths of both approaches, maintaining factual precision while adding interpretive value.

- **Domain-specific adaptation** tailors the summarization approach to specific contexts. This includes scientific data analysis emphasizing methodological precision and statistical validity, intelligence analysis highlighting reliability assessment and confidence levels, business intelligence focusing on actionable implications and decision support, and academic research balancing theoretical integration with empirical evidence. This customization ensures that summaries align with domain-specific standards and requirements, maintaining appropriate rigor while maximizing utility.

Effective implementation typically integrates these approaches tailored to specific analytical requirements, information characteristics, and utilization contexts. The overarching objective remains consistent: transforming the vastness of information into comprehensible and actionable insights while ensuring appropriate fidelity to the source data.

Narrative Construction

Beyond simple condensation, LLMs excel at transforming intricate data into coherent narratives that elucidate system dynamics through storytelling structures. This narrative construction proves particularly valuable for comprehending complex systems:

- **Causal sequencing** organizes events and patterns into logical progression. LLMs can identify initiating conditions that triggered system alterations, trace causal chains through multiple interaction steps, distinguish between proximate and ultimate causes, and recognize feedback loops that amplify or diminish initial effects. This sequencing transforms isolated observations into comprehensible cause-effect relationships, rendering system dynamics intelligible through narrative logic.

- **Actor-centered storytelling** facilitates comprehension by organizing understanding around system participants. LLMs can narrate events from the viewpoint of pivotal agents or subgroups, attribute motivations that elucidate observed behaviors, monitor how agent objectives change through system interactions, and identify conflicts and alignments among various actors. This methodology draws upon our innate human capacity for social comprehension, rendering intricate system dynamics comprehensible through familiar agent-based reasoning.

- **Turning point identification** elucidates pivotal junctures in system evolution. LLMs possess the capability to discern phase transitions between distinct system states, pinpoint decision points that significantly shaped trajectories, discern external shocks that disrupt established patterns, and identify the emergence of novel behavioral patterns or relationship structures. This punctuated narrative facilitates analysts' comprehension of how systems evolve through a combination of gradual change and abrupt transitions, rather than adhering to a uniform progression.

- **Multi-ending scenario development** explores alternative trajectories. LLMs can construct branching narratives depicting diverse potential developments, identify key uncertainties that could lead to divergent outcomes, explore counterfactual scenarios based on alternative decisions, and assess the relative probability of various potential futures. This approach transforms static analysis into dynamic comprehension that supports anticipatory thinking and contingency planning.

Narrative construction draws upon fundamental human cognitive patterns, transforming abstract data into narratives that engage both analytical and intuitive comprehension. This approach renders intricate system dynamics not merely intellectually comprehensible but viscerally comprehensible, thereby facilitating knowledge development and effective communication with diverse stakeholders.

Pattern Interpretation and Explanation

Beyond data summation, LLMs possess pivotal capabilities for pattern interpretation—explanation of observed phenomena, elucidation of their causes, and elucidation of their implications.

This interpretive function transforms pattern recognition into genuine comprehension.

Complex systems often exhibit discernible patterns without immediately apparent causal mechanisms. LLMs facilitate the bridging of this gap by establishing connections between observed patterns and plausible underlying processes:

- **Theory-informed interpretation** establishes empirical patterns within established frameworks. LLMs can establish connections between network structures and theoretical models of relationship formation, relate behavioral clusters to psychological or sociological theories, elucidate emergent phenomena through principles of complex systems, and interpret strategic interactions through game-theoretic mechanisms. This approach grounds observation in theoretical understanding, drawing upon existing knowledge to elucidate novel patterns.

- **Multi-level causal analysis** elucidates mechanisms operating at diverse system scales. LLMs can generate micro-level explanations based on the actions of individual agents, meso-level mechanisms involving interactions among subgroups, macro-level systemic processes that generate emergent properties, and cross-level explanations demonstrating how processes at different levels interact. This multi-level perspective elucidates how rudimentary mechanisms can generate intricate patterns through cross-scale interactions.

- **Alternative mechanism comparison** evaluates competing explanations. LLMs can identify multiple potential mechanisms that could generate observed patterns, assess relative plausibility based on available evidence, suggest distinguishing observations that differentiate between mechanisms, and develop integrated explanations that combine multiple complementary mechanisms. This comparative approach prevents premature commitment to single explanations, maintaining appropriate uncertainty while providing actionable understanding.

- **Anomaly resolution** specifically addresses unexpected or contradictory patterns. LLMs can reconcile observations that appear to violate established principles, identify boundary conditions where normal patterns break down, propose extended or modified mechanisms that accommodate anomalies, and recognize when anomalies suggest fundamental reconceptualization. This focus on explanation gaps often drives the most significant analytical breakthroughs, transforming confusing exceptions into deeper understanding.

By connecting patterns to mechanisms, LLMs assist analysts in moving beyond descriptive understanding ("what is happening") to explanatory comprehension ("why it is happening") is a crucial step for both prediction and intervention in complex systems.

Contextual Interpretation

Patterns in intricate systems gain significance only within appropriate contexts. LLMs excel at contextualizing observations, placing them within relevant historical, cultural, theoretical, and comparative frameworks:

- **Historical contextualization** provides a temporal perspective on current patterns. LLMs can compare present patterns with historical precedents, identify evolutionary trajectories leading to current states, recognize cyclical patterns recurring across time periods, and distinguish novel developments from recurring variations. This temporal context prevents misinterpreting typical fluctuations as significant changes while highlighting genuinely unprecedented developments.

- **Cross-system comparison** places observations within broader experiential knowledge. LLMs can analogize current systems to similar cases with known outcomes, identify pattern variations across different system instances, recognize universal principles versus context-specific manifestations, and leverage insights from well-understood systems to illuminate novel cases. This comparative context facilitates knowledge transfer across domains, preventing analytical siloization while respecting unique system characteristics.

- **Cultural and institutional frameworks** recognize how social contexts shape interpretation. LLMs can identify how cultural frameworks influence agent behaviors, discern institutional constraints shaping interaction patterns, account for how shared beliefs affect coordination mechanisms, and acknowledge how value systems determine objective hierarchies. This social contextualization prevents the misattribution of culturally-specific patterns to universal mechanisms, supporting more accurate causal understanding.

- **Stakeholder perspective integration** considers how different participants interpret the same patterns. LLMs can represent how different agents perceive system dynamics, identify discrepancies between actor interpretations, explain how perspective differences drive strategic interactions, and recognize when misaligned mental models create system dysfunction. This perspective integration acknowledges that participant interpretations directly influence system behavior in social systems, making understanding these interpretations essential for accurate analysis.

Contextual interpretation transforms isolated pattern recognition into meaningful understanding embedded within appropriate reference frames. This context-sensitive approach prevents both overgeneralization (applying universal explanations to context-specific phenomena) and excessive particularization (treating each observation as unique when it exemplifies broader patterns).

Uncertainty Communication

Complex systems inherently involve uncertainty stemming from limited observability, stochastic processes, and fundamental unpredictability. LLMs provide sophisticated capabilities for explicitly communicating uncertainty without compromising analytical value:

- **Confidence level articulation** explicitly represents certainty gradations. LLMs can provide precise probability estimates for quantifiable uncertainties, calibrated verbal expressions for qualitative confidence levels, explicit reasoning chains supporting confidence assessments, and transparent acknowledgment of speculative elements. This calibrated communication effectively prevents both false certainty (presenting speculations as facts) and excessive hedging (undermining valuable insights with overstated caveats).

- **Source reliability assessment** differentiates between various evidence qualities. LLMs can distinguish direct observations from inferred patterns, evaluate the methodological rigor of underlying analyses, acknowledge potential data collection or interpretation biases, and weigh conflicting evidence based on relative credibility. This evidence qualification enables analysts to appropriately weigh different information sources when forming overall judgments.

- **An alternative interpretation of the presentation** acknowledges the explanatory plurality. LLMs can present multiple viable explanations for observed patterns, assess the relative plausibility of alternatives, identify key disagreements between competing interpretations, and suggest specific observations that might resolve uncertainties. This approach prevents premature convergence on single explanations while providing a structured understanding of remaining uncertainties.

- **Known-unknown mapping** explicitly identifies knowledge gaps. LLMs can highlight specific uncertainties most relevant to key conclusions, distinguish between reducible and irreducible uncertainties, suggest targeted data collection to address critical gaps, and acknowledge fundamental limits to predictability. This explicit gap acknowledgment directs attention and resources toward uncertainties with greatest analytical leverage, supporting efficient knowledge development.

Effective uncertainty communication effectively transforms ambiguous uncertainty into a structured understanding of specific knowledge limitations. This process supports appropriate confidence calibration while preserving analytical utility even in the presence of incomplete information—a crucial capability for complex systems analysis where absolute certainty remains permanently elusive.

Hypothesis Generation Through LLMs

Complex systems analysis requires continuous hypothesis development to guide investigation and explain observations. LLMs provide powerful capabilities for generating, refining, and testing hypotheses about system behavior—serving as creative partners that extend human imagination and analytical reach:

- **Abduction** serves as a fundamental reasoning mode for developing hypotheses about intricate systems. LLMs support sophisticated abductive reasoning that bridges observed patterns and potential explanations.

- **Pattern-based hypothesis formation** develops explanations from observed regularities. LLMs can identify consistent relationships between system variables, recognize recurring sequences suggesting causal connections, detect structural similarities across different system components, and notice correlations between seemingly unrelated phenomena. This approach transforms pattern recognition into causal propositions that can guide further investigation.

- **Anomaly-driven hypothesis generation** focuses on explaining unexpected observations. LLMs can identify observations that contradict established understanding, develop explanations that resolve apparent contradictions, propose mechanisms that account for exceptional cases, and suggest extensions to existing theories to accommodate anomalies. This anomaly-focused approach often drives breakthrough insights by highlighting where current understanding falls short.

- **Integration-oriented hypothesis development** fosters the creation of comprehensive explanatory frameworks. LLMs possess the capability to synthesize multiple partial explanations into coherent wholes, identify shared mechanisms underlying disparate phenomena, construct conceptual models that bridge disparate observations, and develop theoretical frameworks with extensive explanatory power. This integrative approach transforms fragmented knowledge into cohesive explanatory structures that elucidate underlying system dynamics.

- **Causal mechanism specification** proposes concrete processes. LLMs can articulate step-by-step causal sequences, identify necessary and sufficient conditions for observed outcomes, specify feedback mechanisms that amplify or regulate effects, and detail interaction processes between system components. This mechanistic focus transforms abstract causal claims into specific, testable propositions about how system components interact to produce observed phenomena.

Abductive reasoning supported by LLMs assists analysts in developing plausible explanations for intricate patterns without being constrained by prior theoretical frameworks or personal experience. This augments analytical imagination while maintaining logical rigor, generating hypotheses that human analysts may overlook due to cognitive biases or knowledge limitations.

Counterfactual Exploration

Understanding intricate systems necessitates contemplating not only the observed outcomes but also the potential outcomes under alternative conditions. LLMs excel at systematic counterfactual reasoning, which explores diverse possibilities:

- **Intervention-based counterfactuals** investigate how systems might respond to modifications. LLMs can analyze the impact of specific policy interventions on outcomes, explore the effects of varying resource allocations or rule structures, examine the influence of targeted information provision on agent decisions, and investigate how removing particular constraints might facilitate novel behaviors. These intervention counterfactuals facilitate both retrospective comprehension and prospective planning by establishing a connection between specific changes and potential system responses.

- **Path dependency analysis** investigates how historical contingencies influence outcomes. LLMs can identify critical junctures where minor variations resulted in significant consequences, explore alternative trajectories that could have emerged from different initial conditions, examine mechanisms that perpetuate historically contingent patterns, and assess whether observed outcomes were inevitable or highly contingent. This historical counterfactual analysis reveals how current system states are dependent on specific developmental paths rather than representing unique equilibria.

- **Structural variant exploration** examines how alternative system architectures might function. LLMs can analyze how alternative network structures affect information flow, explore how different institutional arrangements might alter incentives, consider how alternative coordination mechanisms might influence efficiency, and investigate how different technological infrastructures might shape interactions. These structural counterfactuals assist in distinguishing between outcomes determined by fundamental system architecture versus those resulting from mutable design choices.

- **Systematic assumption** testing systematically varies analytical presuppositions. LLMs can systematically explore how different rationality assumptions affect predicted behaviors, examine the consequences of alternative preference structures, investigate how different information availability would influence decisions, and consider how alternative objective functions might change agent strategies. This presuppositional counterfactual analysis helps identify which assumptions critically determine analytical conclusions versus those with minimal impact.

Counterfactual exploration supported by LLMs expands analytical imagination beyond observed realities while maintaining logical consistency. This helps overcome hindsight bias (the tendency to see historical outcomes as inevitable) and extends analysis beyond the limitations of observed data, supporting both deeper causal understanding and more creative intervention design.

Cross-Domain Analogical Reasoning

Complex systems analysis can benefit from drawing parallels between seemingly disparate domains that share underlying structural similarities. LLMs excel at identifying and exploring these cross-domain analogies:

- **Structure-mapping analogies** identify isomorphic patterns across domains. LLMs can recognize similar network architectures in biological and social systems, identify parallel strategic dynamics across business and diplomatic contexts, map similar feedback mechanisms between ecological and economic systems, and find equivalent coordination challenges in organizational and computational domains. These structural analogies facilitate the transfer of insights across seemingly disparate systems that share fundamental organizational principles.

- **Process-based analogies** focus on similar dynamic patterns. LLMs can connect epidemic spreading to information diffusion processes, relate market bubble dynamics to resource exploitation patterns, link predator-prey cycles to competitive business relationships, and compare technological innovation patterns to biological evolution. These process analogies reveal common temporal dynamics across diverse systems, supporting the transfer of predictive understanding.

- **Function-centered analogies** establish analogous purposes across diverse mechanisms. LLMs can relate various resilience strategies across natural and engineered systems, connect diverse coordination mechanisms serving similar functions, compare different selection processes that yield analogous outcomes, and identify diverse adaptation strategies addressing similar challenges. These functional analogies facilitate the transfer of design principles across domains, inspiring novel approaches based on solutions evolved in distinct contexts.

- **Multi-level analogies** draw parallels at varying system scales. LLMs can connect cell-organism-ecosystem relationships to individual-organization-market dynamics, relate neuron-network-brain hierarchies to person-team-organization structures, map atom-molecule-material relationships to component-module-system architectures, and compare letter-word-text hierarchies to data-information-knowledge relationships. These scale-crossing analogies enable the comprehension of how micro-level interactions manifest macro-level properties across fundamentally disparate systems.

Cross-domain analogical reasoning supported by LLMs significantly expands the knowledge base available for hypothesis generation. By identifying previously overlooked structural similarities between disparate domains, LLMs assist analysts in leveraging insights from well-understood systems to illuminate less familiar ones, thereby overcoming domain silos that might otherwise restrict analytical imagination.

Natural Language Interfaces

Beyond their analytical capabilities, LLMs offer natural language interfaces that revolutionize human interaction with complex systems, data, and models. These interfaces reduce technical barriers, facilitating broader engagement with sophisticated analysis while simultaneously supporting more intuitive exploration of intricate phenomena.

Interactive Exploration Through Dialogue

Traditional analytical tools often require precise technical specifications for queries or commands, which can be challenging for non-specialists. In contrast, LLM-based dialogue interfaces facilitate interactive exploration through natural conversations:

- **Progressive refinement dialogues** support iterative analytical focus. LLMs can initiate broad inquiries to establish context, progressively narrow focus based on emerging insights, adaptively shift attention as intriguing patterns emerge, and seamlessly incorporate feedback and redirection. This conversational approach aligns with human natural exploration of complex topics, following emerging threads of interest rather than adhering to predetermined query paths.

- **Mixed-initiative interaction** strikes a balance between user and system direction. LLMs empower users to direct inquiries through questions and requests, while simultaneously suggesting related explorations. Users can redirect based on specific interests, while the system identifies potential gaps or overlooked dimensions. This harmonious dialogue combines human judgment regarding significance with system capabilities for comprehensive coverage, resulting in more thorough exploration than either could achieve independently.

- **Multi-modal integration** seamlessly combines natural language with other input types. LLMs facilitate verbal references to visual elements ("Tell me more about this cluster."), natural language queries about numerical data ("What's driving this increase?"), conversational interactions with simulations ("What if we doubled this parameter?"), and text-based modifications of network visualizations ("Show me only the high-centrality nodes."). This integration enables seamless transitions between different representation types, combining the precision of specialized formats with the flexibility of natural language.

- **Explanation dialogues** facilitate comprehension through interactive questioning. LLMs empower users to request clarification of intricate concepts, while the system provides explanations tailored to the user's expertise. Users can pose follow-up inquiries directed at specific confusion points, and the system offers alternative explanations when initial explanations prove inadequate. This iterative explanation process closely resembles human teaching interactions, enabling progressive knowledge acquisition rather than relying on one-size-fits-all explanations.

Interactive dialogue interfaces transform analytical systems from technical expertise-requiring tools into collaborative partners accessible to a broader user base. This democratizes access to complex systems analysis while simultaneously supporting more intuitive exploration paths that align more closely with human cognitive processes.

Query Translation and Interpretation

Complex analytical systems necessitate formal language queries with precise syntax. LLMs excel in translating natural language queries into formal queries and interpreting results back into comprehensible language:

- **Intent recognition** identifies the analytical objectives behind questions. LLMs can distinguish between requests for data, explanations, predictions, or recommendations, recognize implied but unstated analytical objectives, identify multiple intents within compound queries, and disambiguate unclear requests through contextual interpretation. This intent focus ensures responses address the underlying analytical needs rather than merely responding to literal query formulations.

- **Query formalization** transforms natural language into precise analytical instructions. LLMs can convert conversational questions into database queries, translate general requests into specific analytical procedures, transform ambiguous terms into well-defined parameters, and expand underspecified requests with appropriate defaults. This translation enables non-technical users to access sophisticated analytical capabilities without mastering formal query languages or statistical procedures.

- **Result interpretation** transforms technical outputs into comprehensible explanations. LLMs can translate statistical results into plain-language conclusions, elucidate the significance of identified patterns, contextualize findings within broader understanding, and highlight practical implications of technical results. This interpretive layer ensures that analytical insights become accessible rather than remaining confined within technical formats comprehensible only to specialists.

- **Iterative refinement** enhances queries through dialogue. LLMs can suggest query modifications to better align with user intentions, propose alternative formulations for ambiguous requests, suggest additional analyses that complement initial queries, and refine interpretation based on user feedback. This iterative process transforms rigid query systems into adaptable exploration tools that evolve with user understanding and objectives.

Query translation capabilities empower non-specialists to utilize sophisticated analytical systems without extensive technical training. This broadens participation in complex systems analysis while ensuring that technical depth remains accessible rather than concealed behind specialized interfaces.

Explanation Generation

Complex systems analysis frequently yields results whose significance may not be immediately apparent, especially to stakeholders lacking technical expertise. LLMs excel in generating explanations that render analytical outcomes comprehensible to a broad spectrum of audiences:

- **Audience-adapted explanations** adjust content to the recipient's level of knowledge. LLMs can provide technical explanations tailored to specialist audiences, while simultaneously simplifying explanations to maintain accuracy for general audiences. Metaphorical explanations facilitate the comprehension of concepts through analogy, and progressive explanations systematically build understanding in stages. This adaptation ensures that explanations provide the appropriate level of detail without overwhelming or underestimating the audience's capabilities.

- **Multilevel causal explanations** elucidate the reasons behind observed patterns. LLMs can generate proximate explanations that address immediate causes, ultimate explanations that identify underlying drivers, mechanism explanations that detail how causes generate effects, and contextual explanations that situate patterns within broader contexts. This causal depth transforms pattern observation into genuine comprehension supporting prediction and intervention.

- **Counterfactual explanations** elucidate significance through contrast. LLMs can elucidate potential outcomes under alternative conditions, identify critical factors influencing outcomes, distinguish necessary from sufficient conditions, and illustrate causal importance through hypothetical scenarios. These contrastive explanations assist audiences in comprehending the salient aspects of intricate situations, directing attention to pivotal drivers rather than extraneous factors.

- **Visual-verbal integration** integrates complementary explanation modalities. LLMs can provide verbal explanations of patterns depicted in visualizations, annotations highlighting pertinent visual elements, narrative sequences guiding attention through complex displays, and conceptual frameworks organizing visual information. This multimodal approach leverages both visual pattern recognition and verbal logical processing, resulting in a more comprehensive understanding than either modality could achieve independently.

Explanation capabilities empower analytical insights to influence decisions and actions by rendering them comprehensible to individuals lacking technical expertise. This bridges the gap between analysis and application, ensuring that the comprehension of complex systems becomes practically useful rather than remaining confined to technical specialists.

Knowledge Graph Integration

Individual analytical techniques offer valuable but fragmented insights into intricate systems. Knowledge graphs, structured representations of entities, relationships, and attributes, facilitate the integration of these fragments into a comprehensive understanding. LLMs provide robust capabilities for constructing, querying, and reasoning with these knowledge structures:

- **Complex systems analysis** generates many disparate knowledge fragments that necessitate integration into cohesive structures. LLMs facilitate the construction of unified knowledge representations that establish connections between these elements.

- **Entity extraction and normalization** identify pivotal system components. LLMs can recognize entities mentioned across multiple documents and data sources, resolve disparate references to the same underlying entities, classify entities into appropriate types and categories, and establish unique identifiers for consistent representation. This foundational approach ensures that knowledge integration is based on accurately identified system components, thereby mitigating the risk of entity confusion.

- **Relationship extraction** identifies connections between entities. LLMs can detect explicit relationship statements in textual data, infer implicit relationships from behavioral patterns, extract relationship attributes such as strength, type, and directionality, and identify temporal dynamics in how relationships evolve. These relationship structures form the connective tissue of knowledge graphs, encoding how system components interact and influence each other.

- **Attribute assignment** captures entity characteristics. LLMs can extract properties mentioned in descriptive texts, convert quantitative measurements into structured attributes, identify attribute changes over time, and resolve contradictory attribute claims from different sources. These attributes provide essential context for understanding entity behaviors and relationship patterns within the system.

- **Ontological organization** establishes structured knowledge frameworks. LLMs can develop classification hierarchies for entity types, establish relationship taxonomies with precise semantics, create property specifications with appropriate value constraints, and construct logical rules that ensure knowledge consistency. This ontological structure transforms collections of facts into organized knowledge systems that support sophisticated querying and inference.

By integrating disparate knowledge fragments into structured representations, LLMs facilitate the transformation of isolated analytical insights into comprehensive system understanding. These integrated knowledge structures support both human comprehension and automated reasoning about intricate system dynamics.

Cross-Domain Knowledge Connection

Complex systems often span multiple knowledge domains, each with their own specialized terminology, concepts, and frameworks. LLMs excel at bridging these domain boundaries by effectively connecting knowledge across them:

- **Terminology alignment** addresses linguistic differences. LLMs can identify equivalent terms used in different domains, establish mappings between specialized vocabularies, resolve polysemy (the existence of multiple meanings for a single term across domains), and develop shared terminology that facilitates cross-domain communication. This linguistic bridge enables knowledge transfer that terminological barriers would otherwise hinder.

- **Conceptual mapping** connects domain-specific frameworks. LLMs can identify structurally equivalent concepts across domains, establish correspondences between theoretical constructs, create translation rules between different analytical frameworks, and highlight conceptual gaps where direct equivalence does not exist. These conceptual connections enable insights from one domain to inform understanding in others, leading to richer, integrated perspectives.

- **Methodological integration** facilitates the seamless integration of diverse analytical approaches. LLMs can establish common underlying phenomena across various measurement approaches, identify complementary analytical techniques, and create multi-method workflows that leverage diverse approaches. Furthermore, LLMs can pinpoint instances where methodological differences yield substantively different results. This methodological bridging effectively addresses analytical silos, where different techniques operate in isolation rather than in mutually beneficial combinations.

- **Cross-domain causal models** establish integrated explanatory frameworks. LLMs can identify causal mechanisms that transcend domain boundaries, connect domain-specific causal models into comprehensive explanations, reconcile seemingly contradictory causal claims from disparate perspectives, and develop multi-level explanations spanning multiple domains. These integrated causal frameworks transform domain-specific partial explanations into a holistic understanding transcending traditional boundaries.

LLMs support cross-domain knowledge connections, which mitigate the fragmentation that often characterizes complex systems analysis.

By bridging specialized knowledge areas, LLMs enable a more comprehensive understanding than any single domain perspective could provide.

Regardless of their comprehensiveness, static knowledge representations offer limited utility without effective exploration capabilities. LLMs empower sophisticated query-based knowledge exploration, transforming static structures into dynamic analytical tools:

- **Natural language query processing** facilitates intuitive knowledge access. LLMs can translate natural questions into formal knowledge graph queries, resolve ambiguous entity references through contextual interpretation, handle complex questions requiring multi-step reasoning, and interpret comparative or superlative questions about system properties. This natural interface eliminates technical barriers to knowledge exploration, enabling direct engagement with system understanding.

- **Multi-hop reasoning** involves traversing connection chains to address intricate queries. LLMs can navigate multiple relationship steps to connect distant entities, identify indirect influence paths between system components, discover unexpected connections through transitive relationships, and reveal hidden dependencies through extended causal chains. This path-based reasoning unveils non-obvious connections inaccessible to approaches focusing solely on direct relationships.

- **Counterfactual knowledge queries** explore alternative scenarios. LLMs can simulate knowledge graph modifications to represent hypothetical changes, trace the propagation of effects through relationship structures, identify entities and relationships most affected by specific changes, and compare alternative modification scenarios to assess their relative impacts. These hypothetical explorations facilitate the comprehension of system sensitivity and response patterns without necessitating formal simulation models.

- **Evidence aggregation** integrates support for specific conclusions. LLMs can collect evidence fragments dispersed throughout the knowledge structure, assess cumulative support for particular hypotheses, identify contradictory evidence necessitating reconciliation, and evaluate overall confidence based on evidence quality and consistency. This evidence-centric approach transforms knowledge graphs from fact repositories into analytical tools supporting reasoned conclusions about intricate inquiries.

Query-based exploration capabilities transform static knowledge structures into dynamic analytical environments that support sophisticated reasoning about complex systems. This interactive engagement with structured knowledge enables analysts to develop a deeper understanding than either unstructured exploration or rigidly pre-defined analyses could provide.

Bridging Disciplinary Boundaries

Complex systems often transcend traditional disciplines, each possessing specialized knowledge, methodologies, and viewpoints. LLMs offer uniquely valuable capabilities for bridging these disciplinary gaps, fostering truly interdisciplinary comprehension.

> *Different disciplines develop specialized languages that facilitate precise communication within their respective domains, but also create barriers to cross-disciplinary understanding.*

Language models (LLMs) excel at translating between these specialized vocabularies:

- **Technical terminology translation** bridges the gap between specialized lexicons. LLMs can establish mappings between equivalent terms across various disciplines, elucidate discipline-specific concepts in more accessible language, identify false cognates where similar terms possess distinct meanings, and establish consistent terminology for interdisciplinary communication. This linguistic translation eliminates fundamental knowledge-sharing barriers that frequently hinder effective cross-disciplinary collaboration.

- **Notation and formalism conversion** bridges representational differences. LLMs can translate mathematical formalisms into equivalent representations, convert between different symbolic systems expressing similar concepts, explain discipline-specific notation in more widely understood terms, and create unified representational frameworks for interdisciplinary work. This representational bridging ensures that formal precision in one discipline becomes accessible to experts from others rather than creating impenetrable barriers.

- **Methodological explanation** clarifies different research approaches. LLMs can explain analytical techniques in terms familiar to different disciplines, clarify assumptions underlying different methodological traditions, translate between qualitative and quantitative research paradigms, and build understanding of different evidence standards across fields. This methodological translation helps experts from different backgrounds appropriately interpret findings from unfamiliar research traditions.

- **Metaphor and analogy development** facilitate the creation of conceptual bridges between disparate fields. LLMs can generate cross-disciplinary analogies that establish connections between unfamiliar and familiar concepts. They can construct metaphorical frameworks that facilitate the translation of specialized knowledge, identify structural parallels between various disciplinary frameworks, and construct conceptual models accessible across disciplinary boundaries. These conceptual bridges transform disciplinary knowledge into comprehensible forms for experts from diverse backgrounds, enabling genuine knowledge transfer rather than merely the substitution of terminology.

Furthermore, LLMs facilitate the translation between specialized languages, thereby addressing the "tower of Babel" problem that often hinders the effective integration of insights from different disciplines studying the same complex systems.

> *Different disciplines develop distinct mental models—cognitive frameworks for comprehending how systems operate.*

LLMs facilitate the integration of these diverse perspectives into a more comprehensive understanding:

- **Model comparison and contrast** elucidate similarities and dissimilarities. LLMs can pinpoint where various disciplinary models concur or diverge, identify complementary aspects that offer distinct insights, clarify where disagreements stem from terminology rather than substance, and identify genuine contradictions that necessitate resolution. This comparative analysis mitigates both premature dismissal of unfamiliar perspectives and uncritical acceptance of disciplinary assumptions, thereby promoting thoughtful integration.

- **Complementary perspective integration** integrates diverse viewpoints. LLMs demonstrate how various models illuminate distinct system aspects, construct integrated frameworks encompassing multiple perspectives, develop synthesis models transcending disciplinary boundaries, and construct multi-level explanations spanning diverse analytical scales. This integrative approach transforms disciplinary models from competitors into complementary perspectives that collectively provide a more comprehensive understanding.

- **Methodological pluralism** supports diverse analytical approaches. LLMs elucidate how different methods reveal different system dimensions, design multi-method research approaches leveraging diverse techniques, integrate findings from various methodological traditions, and reconcile seemingly contradictory results from different methods. This methodological breadth mitigates limitations inherent in any single analytical approach, fostering a more robust understanding through triangulation across methods.

- **Boundary object creation** facilitates the development of concepts with cross-disciplinary utility. LLMs can generate meaningful shared models across various fields, establish consistent terminology, create visualizations accessible to diverse expert audiences, and compose narratives that integrate multiple disciplinary perspectives. These boundary objects serve as intellectual meeting points where experts from different backgrounds can engage with shared understanding despite their diverse disciplinary foundations.

By integrating multiple mental models, LLMs help overcome the cognitive fragmentation that often characterizes complex systems analysis. This integrated understanding enables more comprehensive approaches to system modeling, prediction, and intervention than any single disciplinary perspective could provide.

CHAPTER 10

Unified Goal Analysis

Having explored methodologies for comprehending system components, relationships, and interactions in previous chapters, we now focus on perhaps the most critical dimension of complex multi-agent systems: the goals that drive system behavior. Every complex system composed of independent actors ultimately serves some purpose, either by design or emergence. Composing this purpose into component objectives, evaluating how different subgroups contribute, measuring alignment, analyzing feedback mechanisms, and designing appropriate performance metrics provide essential insight into why systems function as they do.

Unified Goal Analysis represents the process of comprehending how individual agent objectives aggregate into collective outcomes and how these outcomes relate to the system's overarching purpose. This analysis proves particularly challenging because goals often remain implicit rather than explicit, may conflict across different system levels, evolve over time, and sometimes produce unintended consequences that become purposes in themselves.

> *Without understanding these goal structures, we cannot fully comprehend why complex systems behave as they do or how they might be influenced.*

This chapter delves into methodologies for analyzing goal structures within intricate systems. We explore techniques for decomposing overarching goals into actionable components, assessing the contributions of various subgroups to goal attainment, measuring alignment between individual and collective objectives, analyzing feedback mechanisms that guide goal direction, and designing performance metrics that monitor progress. Throughout, we underscore the integration of goal analysis with the behavioral, strategic, and structural perspectives developed in preceding chapters.

Decomposing Overall Goals into Manageable Sub-Goals

Complex systems rarely pursue singular, monolithic objectives. Instead, they typically serve multiple related goals organized in hierarchical structures. Decomposing these overall purposes into component sub-goals clarifies system functions and reveals potential tensions or synergies between different objectives.

Understanding intricate systems necessitates identifying both the ultimate objectives and the intermediate objectives that support them. Goal hierarchy analysis elucidates these relationships, establishing a structured representation of how system purposes cascade from high-level outcomes to specific actions.

At the highest level, complex systems typically serve fundamental purposes that justify their existence. A healthcare system, for instance, aims to enhance population health outcomes. A financial market exists to efficiently allocate capital while effectively managing risk. An educational system develops human capabilities and transfers knowledge across generations. These ultimate goals provide the foundation for evaluating system performance and comprehending evolutionary pressures.

Below these ultimate goals lie supporting objectives that facilitate their achievement. For example, a healthcare system's population health goal depends on objectives, such as disease prevention, effective treatment, equitable access, and sustainable resource management. These second-level goals remain outcome-focused but more specific, establishing a bridge between abstract ultimate purposes and concrete activities.

Further decomposition yields increasingly specific objectives that directly guide system behaviors. Disease prevention encompasses vaccination programs, health education, environmental protection, and early screening initiatives. Each of these components represents a distinct functional area with dedicated resources, specialized expertise, and specific metrics while maintaining clear connections to higher-level purposes.

Effective goal hierarchies possess several key characteristics. First, they demonstrate comprehensiveness, ensuring that all essential system functions receive recognition. Second, they maintain clear vertical alignment, with each sub-goal demonstrating a logical connection to higher-level objectives. Third, they strike a balance between breadth and depth, providing sufficient granularity to guide specific actions without becoming excessively complex. Finally, they acknowledge both explicit goals (formally recognized system purposes) and implicit goals (unstated objectives revealed through resource allocation and decision patterns).

Developing accurate goal hierarchies typically involves integrating multiple information sources. Formal documentation, such as mission statements, strategic plans, policy documents, and charters, provides explicit goal articulations. Behavioral analysis reveals implicit priorities through resource allocation, attention patterns, and decision criteria. Stakeholder interviews capture diverse perspectives on system purposes, often uncovering goals not formally acknowledged. Historical analysis traces how objectives have evolved over time, distinguishing persistent core purposes from transient priorities.

The resulting goal hierarchy serves as a comprehensive framework for comprehending system behavior at various levels. It elucidates potential conflicts between disparate objectives, identifies deficiencies where crucial goals lack supporting mechanisms, and establishes a common reference point for diverse stakeholders to discuss system objectives. Furthermore, it facilitates the transformation of abstract objectives into tangible components that can be specifically addressed through intervention or redesign.

Interdependency Mapping

While hierarchical representations effectively illustrate vertical relationships among objectives, they often neglect to capture horizontal interdependencies among objectives at the same level. Interdependency mapping serves as a complementary analysis approach, investigating how various objectives influence each other, thereby uncovering synergies, conflicts, and intricate feedback mechanisms.

Certain goal relationships exhibit positive synergies, where progress toward one objective naturally facilitates the advancement of others. For instance, in educational systems, student engagement improvements typically enhance knowledge acquisition and social development. Similarly, in economic systems, productivity growth often supports both business profitability and worker income. These synergistic relationships establish virtuous cycles where initial progress in one area catalyzes improvements across multiple objectives.

Conversely, many intricate systems harbor objectives with adverse interdependencies, wherein advancing one objective impedes others. Healthcare systems encounter fundamental conflicts between cost containment and treatment innovation, with cutting-edge therapies frequently resulting in elevated expenses. Transportation systems strive to balance accessibility, speed, safety, and environmental impact, frequently discovering that optimizing any single dimension compromises others. These negative interdependencies necessitate strategic trade-offs that require thoughtful prioritization rather than simplistic maximization.

The most intricate goal relationships involve conditional dependencies, wherein the relationship between objectives evolves based on circumstances or developmental stages.

Economic growth and environmental protection often exhibit such conditional interdependencies—at certain development stages and with specific technologies, they function as competing objectives. At the same time, in other contexts, they can become mutually reinforcing through sustainable development approaches. These conditional relationships necessitate a sophisticated understanding of context factors determining whether particular goal combinations yield positive or negative interactions.

Temporal dependencies introduce a further layer of complexity, with varying goal relationships dominating different time horizons. Numerous systems exhibit short-term trade-offs that subsequently transform into long-term synergies. Investments in preventive healthcare initially incur higher costs but ultimately reduce treatment expenses. Similarly, educational system investments exhibit similar temporal patterns, with upfront costs yielding long-term social benefits. Recognizing these temporal dimensions is crucial to avoid short-sighted decisions prioritizing immediate over long-term system objectives.

Effective interdependency mapping utilizes several complementary techniques. Cross-impact analysis systematically examines how progress in each goal area affects all others, creating a comprehensive relationship matrix. Causal loop diagrams visualize feedback relationships, identifying reinforcing and balancing loops that connect different objectives. System dynamics modeling quantifies these relationships, enabling simulation of how interventions targeting specific goals propagate through the system. Qualitative research captures stakeholder understanding of goal interactions, incorporating experiential knowledge about how objectives interact in practice.

The resulting interdependency map transforms one-dimensional goal lists into a multidimensional understanding of how objectives form interconnected systems. This perspective reveals leverage points where interventions might create positive cascades across multiple goals. It identifies potential unintended consequences when the single-minded pursuit of particular objectives undermines others. Perhaps most importantly, it enables thoughtful navigation of necessary trade-offs, supporting deliberate decisions about priority balancing rather than allowing unconscious assumptions to determine which goals receive precedence.

Complex systems rarely maintain static purposes. Instead, their objectives evolve over time in response to changing environments, internal development, and feedback from past performance. Understanding this temporal evolution provides crucial insight into both current functioning and likely future directions.

Many complex systems exhibit developmental trajectories with predictable goal evolution patterns. Early development phases typically emphasize existence goals focused on establishing core functionality and securing necessary resources. As systems mature, they shift toward stability objectives to maintain reliable operations and protect established capabilities. Mature systems eventually develop enhancement goals to optimize performance, expand capabilities, or address higher-order needs. These evolutionary patterns explain why similar systems at different developmental stages prioritize dramatically different objectives despite ostensibly serving the same ultimate purpose.

External context shifts drive another dimension of goal evolution. Environmental changes, such as technological advancements, demographic shifts, resource availability alterations, or competitive landscape transformations, alter the viability and significance of various objectives. Financial systems underwent a significant transformation following the 2008 crisis, prioritizing stability objectives previously subordinated to growth and innovation. Similarly, healthcare systems were reprioritized during the COVID-19 pandemic, temporarily subordinating efficiency and cost-containment to surge capacity and rapid response capabilities. These context-driven evolution patterns emphasize that system purposes remain contingent on external conditions rather than representing immutable qualities.

Internal learning processes establish a third evolutionary mechanism, whereby systems modify their objectives in response to experience. Initial objectives frequently prove inadequate, unrealistic, or imbalanced, necessitating refinement through operational feedback. Novel objectives emerge as system participants recognize unrecognized opportunities or requirements. Existing objectives undergo transformation as comprehension deepens regarding the specific outcomes that align with broader purposes. These learning-based evolutions constitute healthy adaptation when they reflect genuine insight, although they can also manifest as goal displacement when the means gradually become the ends themselves.

Across these evolutionary patterns, effective goal systems maintain a balance between stability and adaptability. Core purposes provide continuity even as specific objectives evolve, creating a sense of persistent identity despite changing priorities. Nested timeframes allow simultaneous pursuit of short-term operational goals, medium-term developmental objectives, and long-term aspirational purposes. Explicit revision processes provide structured opportunities to reconsider objectives in light of new information while preventing destabilizing constant change.

Analyzing temporal goal evolution necessitates a comprehensive approach that integrates historical perspective and future orientation. Historical analysis elucidates the evolution of system objectives, identifying patterns of development, responses to past context shifts, and learning-based refinements. Contemporary analysis scrutinizes present transitional indicators, acknowledging emerging goals that may not yet be formally recognized and gradually de-prioritizing declining priorities. Future projection contemplates anticipated environmental changes, impending developmental transitions, and potential learning opportunities that could catalyze further evolution.

This temporal perspective transforms static goal analysis into a dynamic understanding of how system purposes evolve. It establishes realistic expectations for future developments, identifying potential priority shifts before they become formalized. It distinguishes between temporary goal adjustments in response to unusual circumstances and fundamental purpose evolution, representing permanent directional change. Perhaps most significantly, it supports intentional management of goal evolution rather than allowing purposes to drift through unconscious adaptation or unrecognized displacement.

Evaluating Subgroup Contributions

Complex systems attain their overall objectives through the collective contributions of diverse subgroups, each performing distinct roles in pursuing goals. By comprehending these differential contributions, we gain insights into the interactions between system components, enabling us to discern both critical dependencies and potential redundancies.

Every complex system distributes goal-advancing functions across various subgroups, establishing a division of labor that facilitates specialized contributions toward collective objectives. Functional role analysis elucidates this distribution, mapping how distinct system components contribute to specific facets of the overarching goal structure.

Certain subgroups directly advance the ultimate system objectives through frontline activities. For instance, in healthcare systems, clinical providers directly enhance patient outcomes through diagnostic, therapeutic, and preventive services. Similarly, in educational systems, teachers directly advance learning objectives through instructional activities. These frontline functional roles maintain the most direct connection to the ultimate system objectives, although they typically rely on supporting functions to ensure their effectiveness.

Other subgroups serve enabling functions that create the necessary conditions for direct goal advancement. Information technology groups enable modern healthcare delivery by maintaining essential data systems. Administrative staff enable educational achievement by managing resources, schedules, and facilities. While these enabling functions may appear distant from ultimate purposes when viewed in isolation, they prove essential for sustainable goal achievement, creating the infrastructural foundation upon which direct activities depend.

Governance functions comprise a third crucial category, providing direction, coordination, and accountability. Executive leadership, boards, and regulatory bodies establish priorities, allocate resources, resolve conflicts, and evaluate performance. Although these functions may appear even further removed from front-line activities, they maintain systemic alignment with ultimate purposes, preventing drift toward suboptimal equilibria or capture by interests inconsistent with overall system goals.

Adaptive functions constitute a fourth fundamental category dedicated to system evolution and enhancement. Research and development units, quality improvement teams, and innovation initiatives contribute to long-term goal achievement by developing novel capabilities, addressing emerging challenges, and optimizing efficiency. While these functions may not directly advance immediate objectives, they prove pivotal for sustained effectiveness in dynamic environments.

Effective complex systems maintain dynamic equilibrium across these functional domains. Overemphasis on front-line activities without adequate supporting infrastructure leads to unsustainable performance that deteriorates as supporting systems fail.

Excessive investment in enabling functions without corresponding direct activities results in well-supported systems that achieve limited outcomes. Governance overreach creates bureaucratic systems where coordination costs exceed production benefits. Adaptive function neglect generates short-term optimization at the expense of long-term viability.

A multilevel analysis approach is necessary to comprehend this functional distribution. This analysis integrates structural examinations, process tracing, and outcome attribution. Structural analysis elucidates formal responsibility distributions, resource allocations, and authority relationships. Process tracing scrutinizes the flow of specific goal-advancing activities across organizational boundaries, thereby revealing actual functional contributions that may diverge from formal designations. Outcome attribution evaluates how various subgroups influence key performance indicators, quantifying their relative contribution to prioritized objectives.

From a functional perspective, abstract organizational structures are transformed into purposeful activity systems with well-defined goal relationships. This approach emphasizes the critical interdependencies among various functional types, ensuring that direct activities are not prioritized without adequate supporting capabilities. It also identifies potential functional gaps where essential goal-advancing activities lack sufficient support. Furthermore, it establishes a clear connection between each system component and its ultimate purpose, enabling every participant to comprehend their contribution to collective objectives, regardless of their proximity to front-line activities.

Contribution Measurement Approaches

While functional analysis elucidates the theoretical contributions of distinct subgroups to goal attainment, empirical measurement furnishes concrete evidence regarding the nature and extent of these contributions. Several complementary approaches facilitate rigorous evaluation of how various system components contribute to realizing collective objectives.

> *Counterfactual analysis stands out as a conceptually potent approach, investigating the potential impact of removing, modifying, or enhancing specific subgroups on the achievement of goals.*

Natural experiments, which arise from external factors creating variations in subgroup presence or capacity, offer opportunities for such analysis without the need for deliberate intervention. For instance, a regional healthcare provider strike serves as a natural experiment for assessing their contribution to health outcomes. Similarly, a temporary technology system failure illuminates the role of information infrastructure in organizational performance. These natural variations enable the measurement of how outcome indicators evolve when specific functions become unavailable.

In instances where natural experiments prove infeasible, simulation models emerge as alternative avenues for counterfactual assessment. Agent-based models simulate the dynamics of system performance under diverse subgroup configurations. System dynamics models delve into the impact of modifying specific functions on goal-relevant outcomes. These simulation approaches, while inherently simplified, provide structured exploration of contribution patterns that may be challenging to discern directly:

- **Process tracing methodologies** offer a complementary approach that focuses on how subgroup activities are connected to measurable outcomes through causal chains. These methods identify critical intermediate outcomes produced by different system components and establish plausible links between these intermediate and ultimate goal achievement. Process tracing proves particularly valuable for understanding enabling and governance functions whose contributions manifest indirectly through multiple causal steps rather than directly influencing final outcomes.

- **Value attribution techniques** provide quantitative approaches for distributing credit for goal achievement across contributing subgroups. Statistical methods such as structural equation modeling or path analysis quantify how different variables influence outcomes of interest. Economic approaches such as Shapley value allocation distribute credit based on marginal contribution principles. These quantitative techniques transform subjective contribution assessment into measurable attribution, although they require careful interpretation given the inherent interconnectedness of complex system activities.

- **Stakeholder perception assessment** provides a comprehensive approach that integrates expert judgment regarding contribution patterns. Structured interviews, surveys, or Delphi processes gather informed opinions about how various subgroups contribute to collective goals. These perception-based approaches leverage system participants' tacit knowledge acquired through direct experience, capturing insights that are challenging to measure through more objective methodologies.

- **Effective contribution measurement** typically involves integrating multiple approaches, triangulating across different methodologies to develop a robust understanding. Quantitative attribution provides numerical precision but may overlook nuanced relationships. Qualitative process tracing captures causal complexity but struggles with precise contribution quantification. Stakeholder perceptions incorporate tacit knowledge but may reflect biases or limited perspectives. By combining these approaches, analysts can develop a more comprehensive understanding of how different system components contribute to collective purposes.

This empirical perspective transforms abstract functional mapping into evidence-based contribution assessment. It identifies high-leverage subgroups whose enhancement would significantly advance goal achievement. It reveals underappreciated functions whose contributions exceed their recognized value. It highlights potential efficiency opportunities where resource investments yield suboptimal goal advancement. Perhaps most importantly, it provides an objective foundation for resource allocation decisions, ensuring investments flow toward functions with demonstrated contribution to priority objectives.

Gap and Redundancy Identification

Complex systems necessitate both comprehensive coverage of all essential goal-advancing functions and appropriate redundancy for critical activities. Gap and redundancy analysis evaluates whether system components collectively provide the necessary and sufficient capability to advance defined objectives while maintaining adequate resilience against component failure.

Functional gaps arise when essential goal-advancing activities lack adequate support from existing system components. Some gaps manifest as complete absence, where necessary functions lack a responsible subgroup or resource allocation. More commonly, gaps appear as insufficient capacity, where responsible subgroups exist but lack adequate resources, authority, or capability to fully perform the required functions. Subtler gaps emerge when functions receive technically adequate resources but insufficient priority or attention, effectively creating de facto gaps despite nominal coverage.

These gaps typically originate from various mechanisms. Emerging objectives frequently lack established support structures, leading to transitional gaps as systems adapt to new objectives. Boundary functions spanning multiple domains often experience responsibility ambiguity, with each potentially responsible party if others will address shared requirements. Legacy structures designed for previous priorities may persist despite changing needs, resulting in misalignment between current goals and existing functional distributions. Resource constraints necessitate explicit or implicit prioritization, sometimes leaving lower-priority functions with acknowledged but accepted gaps.

Systematic gap identification integrates a diverse range of analytical methodologies. Goal-function mapping scrutinizes each objective to discern supporting functions and their respective subgroups. Performance analysis identifies objectives with insufficient progress, potentially indicating functional gaps. Stakeholder consultation unveils perceived coverage deficiencies based on operational experience. Future scenario exploration anticipates potential gaps emerging as circumstances change, facilitating proactive capability development rather than reactive gap remediation.

While eliminating gaps enhances baseline functionality, complex systems also necessitate appropriate redundancy for critical functions to maintain resilience against component failure. Unlike gaps, which unequivocally represent deficiencies, redundancy assessment involves balancing efficiency against reliability. Excessive redundancy consumes resources and presents coordination challenges, while insufficient redundancy exposes essential functions to single-point failures.

Effective redundancy analysis considers several factors when determining appropriate duplication levels. Function criticality, which quantifies the severity of goal achievement impairment from functional failure, serves as the primary consideration, with more critical functions warranting greater redundancy.

Failure likelihood significantly influences redundancy requirements, with less reliable components necessitating stronger backup capabilities. Recovery timeframes also impact redundancy decisions; functions requiring immediate restoration necessitate standby capacity, while those allowing longer recovery can rely on surge capabilities. Resource intensity shapes practical redundancy limits; costly functions justify more sophisticated reliability approaches than simple duplication.

Several redundancy strategies provide alternatives to simple functional duplication. Degraded continuity plans maintain essential functionality at reduced performance levels during primary system disruptions. Temporary substitution arrangements enable less specialized resources to perform critical functions briefly during emergencies. Mutual aid agreements establish shared redundancy across multiple systems, providing backup without necessitating each system to maintain independent reserve capacity. These approaches often offer more cost-effective resilience than complete function duplication.

Gap and redundancy analysis transform ideal goal structures into practical capability requirements. It ensures that every essential function supporting priority objectives receives adequate resources while maintaining appropriate reliability for critical activities. It identifies opportunity costs where redundancy investments might yield greater returns if redirected toward gap filling. Perhaps most importantly, it creates explicit, evidence-based decisions about acceptable risks and necessary protections, replacing implicit assumptions with deliberate design choices about system resilience.

Measuring Goal Alignment

Complex systems attain optimal performance when the activities of their constituent components are aligned with their overall objectives. However, in systems composed of independent actors, individual objectives may diverge from collective goals, leading to misalignment that compromises system effectiveness. Measuring this alignment and understanding where individual incentives support or undermine collective purposes provides crucial insights into system function and potential improvement opportunities.

> *Within intricate systems, independent actors pursue their own objectives, which may converge, diverge, or directly conflict with the collective objectives.*

By comprehending these alignment patterns, we can elucidate the reasons behind actors' behaviors and how they collectively manifest into system-level outcomes:

- **Perfect alignment** occurs when individual success directly propels collective goals, establishing a harmonious convergence between actor incentives and system objectives. Sales professionals whose compensation is directly tied to customer satisfaction exemplify such alignment—their individual success (earning commissions) necessitates advancing the collective goal (customer satisfaction). Similarly, academic researchers whose career advancement hinges on knowledge contributions that advance their field's collective purpose also exhibit alignment. These aligned situations foster self-sustaining systems where individual self-interest naturally drives collective goal achievement.

- **Partial alignment** exists when individual and collective objectives overlap significantly but not completely. Healthcare providers typically exhibit such partial alignment—their professional satisfaction depends substantially on patient outcomes (supporting collective goals) but also on autonomy, income, and work conditions that may sometimes conflict with system-level objectives like cost containment. These partially aligned situations function adequately most of the time but may produce tensions when the non-aligned aspects of individual objectives influence decisions.

- **Neutral independence** occurs when individual objectives neither advance nor undermine collective purposes. Support functions motivated primarily by professional standards rather than ultimate system outcomes often exhibit such neutrality. Their work maintains adequate quality due to professional pride rather than commitment to system goals, creating reliable but uninspired performance. These neutral situations miss potential synergies from stronger alignment but avoid the active dysfunction of misaligned incentives.

- **Active misalignment** occurs when individual success metrics conflict with collective objectives, leading to fundamental tensions between personal and system goals. Financial advisors compensated based on transaction volume rather than client outcomes exemplify this misalignment, where personal incentives may encourage excessive trading that negatively impacts client financial performance. Misalignment can also manifest when performance metrics reward behaviors that contradict the ultimate system purposes. These misaligned situations inevitably lead to dysfunction unless they are counterbalanced by other factors, such as professional ethics or intrinsic motivation.

Measuring alignment necessitates comparing individual motivational drivers with system-level goal structures. Incentive analysis evaluates formal reward systems, elucidating the relationship between compensation, promotion, recognition, and other extrinsic motivators with collective objectives. Behavioral observation assesses actual decision patterns, uncovering revealed preferences that may diverge from stated priorities. Value and attitude assessment delves into intrinsic motivational factors such as professional identity, personal values, and organizational commitment that influence alignment beyond formal incentives. Attribution analysis examines how individuals rationalize their own successes and failures, providing insights into their operational understanding of what drives outcomes.

This alignment perspective transforms abstract discussions of organizational culture or values into concrete assessments of how individual decision drivers relate to collective objectives. It elucidates why well-intentioned actors sometimes make decisions that undermine system goals, emphasizing that structural incentives rather than personal failings often drive misalignment. It identifies opportunities for recalibrating reward systems or decision criteria to more effectively harmonize individual and collective objectives. Perhaps most significantly, it focuses organizational development efforts on creating conditions where achieving success and accomplishing good become synonymous—where successful individual performance naturally advances collective purposes.

Machine Learning for Goal Alignment

As complex systems generate increasingly detailed data about both individual behaviors and collective outcomes, machine learning approaches provide powerful new tools for measuring goal alignment with unprecedented precision and accuracy. These techniques transform alignment assessment from periodic, sample-based approximations into continuous, comprehensive measurements.

> *Supervised learning algorithms can discern behavioral patterns that predict the attainment of ultimate objectives, thereby constructing empirically derived models of the activities that actually contribute to system purposes.*

These models necessitate training datasets that establish a correlation between observable behaviors and outcome measures, which are typically generated through historical analysis of cases with predetermined outcomes. Upon training, these models can evaluate the alignment of current behaviors with patterns historically associated with goal achievement, thereby providing real-time feedback on the potential contribution to collective objectives.

The most sophisticated applications of alignment combine multiple algorithms targeting different aspects of alignment. Classification algorithms categorize activities into those supporting, neutral to, or potentially undermining collective goals. Regression models quantify the expected magnitude of specific behaviors' contributions to ultimate outcomes. Time-series prediction estimates how current activities will influence future goal measures based on observed temporal relationships. Ensemble methods integrate these perspectives into comprehensive alignment assessments more accurately than any single analytical approach.

These machine learning approaches offer several advantages over traditional alignment measurement. They capture complex, non-linear relationships between behaviors and outcomes that might elude conventional analysis. They continuously improve as new data becomes available, automatically updating alignment models to reflect evolving relationships. They identify unexpected alignment patterns not anticipated in deductive frameworks, revealing counterintuitive connections between specific activities and ultimate goals. Perhaps most importantly, they provide objective, evidence-based assessments minimally influenced by political considerations or conventional wisdom that often distorts traditional alignment evaluation.

Practical implementation typically involves several stages. Initial exploration applies algorithms to historical data, identifying behavioral patterns that best predicted goal advancement in the past. Validation tests these models against separate data not used during training, ensuring that they capture genuine relationships rather than statistical artifacts. Deployment integrates validated models into operational systems that continuously assess current activities against empirically-derived alignment patterns. Ongoing refinement periodically retrains models with new data, maintaining accuracy as system relationships evolve.

While these approaches are powerful, they require careful implementation to avoid several potential pitfalls. Training data quality fundamentally determines model accuracy, making careful outcome measurement and comprehensive behavioral data collection essential. Algorithm selection significantly influences what patterns receive recognition, requiring thoughtful matching of mathematical approaches to alignment questions. Interpretation remains crucial, with human experts needed to distinguish correlation from causation and evaluate whether identified patterns represent genuine alignment rather than confounded relationships.

When effectively implemented, machine learning transforms the abstract concept of goal alignment into a tangible reality.

It establishes an empirical basis for discussions previously characterized by opinion or authority assertions. It identifies specific behaviors most strongly associated with goal advancement, facilitating targeted performance enhancement. Furthermore, it unveils previously unrecognized alignment patterns, broadening our comprehension of how various activities contribute to overarching objectives. Perhaps most significantly, it establishes a learning system where alignment measurement continuously improves, incorporating novel insights and adapting to evolving dynamics between behaviors and outcomes.

Beyond measuring current alignment, comprehending the feedback mechanisms that sustain or modify alignment over time provides invaluable insights into system dynamics. Feedback loop analysis elucidates how systems identify alignment anomalies, respond to misalignment, and evolve toward a more harmonious convergence of individual and collective objectives.

Effective alignment systems integrate multiple feedback mechanisms that operate at various time scales. Real-time feedback provides immediate information about how specific decisions align with established objectives, enabling continuous course correction. Periodic review processes assess alignment patterns across multiple decisions and longer timeframes, identifying systemic issues that may be invisible in transaction-level analysis. Strategic evaluation examines fundamental alignment between organizational structures and ultimate purposes, potentially triggering more substantial realignment when necessary.

These feedback mechanisms are contingent upon specific organizational capabilities. Measurement systems must capture both individual activities and their contribution to collective outcomes, establishing the data foundation for alignment assessment. Interpretation processes must transform raw data into comprehensible insights regarding alignment strengths and weaknesses. Communication channels must convey these insights to relevant decision-makers with sufficient context for informed responses. Adjustment mechanisms must facilitate practical modifications to enhance identified misalignments, ensuring that feedback is diagnostic and therapeutic.

Several prevalent failure patterns impede the effectiveness of alignment feedback. Measurement gaps occur when critical activities or outcomes remain untracked, resulting in blind spots in alignment comprehension. Delayed feedback arises when excessive time elapses between activities and their outcome measurement, disrupting the psychological connection necessary for effective learning. Attenuated signals emerge when feedback traverses multiple interpretation layers, potentially distorting or diluting the original insights. Cultural barriers manifest when organizational norms discourage acknowledging or addressing alignment issues, creating environments where feedback exists but remains ineffective.

Beyond these general patterns, specific feedback typologies characterize different system types. Market-based systems primarily rely on economic feedback, with financial outcomes signaling alignment between individual activities and valued outcomes. Professional systems emphasize peer assessment feedback, using colleague evaluations to maintain alignment with field standards and purposes. Hierarchical organizations utilize supervisory feedback, with authority figures assessing and correcting alignment issues. Network-based systems employ distributed reputation feedback, using collective assessment to identify and reward alignment with shared objectives.

Each of these distinct feedback approaches brings unique strengths and limitations. Economic feedback provides clear, objective signals but often captures only outcomes with readily available monetary valuation. Peer assessment incorporates sophisticated qualitative judgment but may suffer from collegial reluctance to provide negative feedback. Supervisory feedback enables decisive correction but relies heavily on individual manager capability and attention. Reputation-based feedback leverages collective wisdom but sometimes amplifies popular misconceptions rather than accurately assessing alignment.

Most effective complex systems employ balanced feedback portfolios that integrate multiple mechanisms to overcome individual limitations.

These systems maintain alignment across various timeframes through layered feedback systems that address immediate, intermediate, and long-term alignment. They combine qualitative and quantitative feedback approaches to compensate for each other's shortcomings. These systems integrate formal feedback structures and informal mechanisms, acknowledging that official systems rarely capture all alignment dimensions.

This feedback perspective transforms static alignment assessments into a dynamic understanding of how systems maintain and enhance harmony between individual and collective objectives. It elucidates why some misalignments persist despite recognition, while others resolve swiftly through effective feedback mechanisms. It identifies specific feedback enhancements that augment system capability for detecting and addressing alignment issues. Perhaps most importantly, it focuses improvement efforts on developing learning capacity that enables continuous alignment enhancement rather than treating alignment as a static state to be achieved once and thereafter maintained unchanged.

Analyzing Feedback Loops and Self-Correction

Complex systems maintain goal direction through feedback processes that detect deviations and initiate corrective actions. Understanding these self-correction mechanisms—how systems identify and respond to performance gaps—provides crucial insights into resilience, adaptability, and improvement capacity.

Before systems can rectify deviations from goal-aligned behavior, they must identify their existence. Effective detection mechanisms continuously monitor system performance, providing timely and accurate awareness of alignment with desired objectives.

Formal performance measurement systems are the most prominent detection mechanism in numerous complex systems. These structured approaches define key indicators aligned with priority objectives, establish measurement methodologies, collect data at predetermined intervals, and compare results against expectations or benchmarks. Well-designed measurement systems balance comprehensiveness and practicality, encompassing all critical goal dimensions while maintaining manageable data collection requirements. They incorporate leading indicators that anticipate potential issues before they fully materialize, alongside lagging measures that confirm ultimate outcome achievement. These systems combine quantitative metrics for precise tracking with qualitative assessments that capture dimensions defensible against simple numerical representation.

While essential, formal measurement systems inevitably contain blind spots where important variables remain untracked. Informal detection mechanisms provide crucial complementary awareness through less structured approaches. Front-line observation by system participants often identifies emerging issues before they register in formal metrics. Stakeholder feedback provides an external perspective on performance dimensions that may receive insufficient internal attention. Narrative information—stories, case examples, and anecdotes—offers rich contextual understanding beyond what metrics alone can provide. These informal mechanisms enhance detection capability but require deliberate attention and legitimization to prevent their insights from being dismissed as merely subjective or anecdotal.

Beyond current performance tracking, effective detection requires appropriate comparison references to interpret measured results. Some systems utilize historical trends as primary references, focusing on whether performance improves or deteriorates over time. Others emphasize external benchmarks, comparing results against peer organizations or established standards. The most sophisticated approaches incorporate trajectory analysis, examining current position and the rate and direction of change relative to desired future states. These comparative frameworks transform raw performance data into meaningful evaluative insights about how the system achieves its objectives.

Detection timing significantly influences correction effectiveness, with earlier awareness enabling more timely, less disruptive adjustments. Real-time monitoring systems immediately detect critical variables where rapid response is essential. Periodic review processes balance comprehensive assessment with practical resource requirements for measures where continuous monitoring proves unnecessary or infeasible. Predictive detection represents the most advanced approach, using early indicators and trend analysis to anticipate performance issues before they fully manifest, enabling preventive rather than merely reactive correction.

Error sensitivity, which quantifies the acceptable deviation from expected performance before triggering detection, is another crucial dimension in detection systems. Some systems employ stringent tolerance approaches, detecting and responding to even minor deviations from anticipated performance. Conversely, others adopt broader tolerance methods, initiating a response only when deviations exceed predefined thresholds representing significant departure from acceptable performance. Adaptive sensitivity provides the most sophisticated approach, dynamically adjusting detection thresholds based on contextual factors such as risk level, improvement stage, or environmental conditions.

These detection capabilities determine the speed and accuracy with which systems recognize performance gaps necessitating correction.

> *Without effective detection, even well-designed response mechanisms remain ineffective, unable to address issues concealed within system awareness. Conversely, highly sensitive detection only holds value when accompanied by appropriate correction capabilities to address the problems identified.*

Correction Response Patterns

Systems must promptly initiate corrective actions to restore goal alignment upon detecting performance deviations. Several distinct response patterns characterize how different systems adjust their behavior when performance gaps emerge:

- **Negative feedback correction** represents the most fundamental pattern, directly counteracting detected deviations to maintain stable performance. When systems observe results below targets, negative feedback augments the effort or resources allocated to underperforming areas. Conversely, when results exceed requirements, such systems may reallocate effort toward other priorities. This straightforward correction approach effectively maintains performance within acceptable ranges in stable environments and well-understood processes. However, it tends toward mediocrity rather than excellence, driving only sufficient improvement to eliminate negative deviations without elevating performance to optimal levels.

- **Amplifying feedback** generates more dynamic correction by intensifying the response to initial signals. Small performance gaps trigger disproportionately strong responses, enabling rapid adjustments that can overcome inertia or resistance. This approach is valuable for breaking out of suboptimal equilibria or responding to emerging crises that necessitate decisive action. However, amplifying feedback carries the risk of overreaction, potentially leading to oscillating performance due to excessive corrections requiring subsequent counter-adjustments. Effective implementation necessitates carefully calibrating amplification factors and applying this approach only in situations requiring intensive response.

- **Learning-based correction** transcends simple adjustments to modify underlying processes based on performance feedback. Rather than merely increasing effort within existing approaches, learning systems analyze the reasons behind performance gaps and revise fundamental methods. This approach fosters sustainable improvement rather than temporary corrections, addressing root causes rather than symptoms. However, it demands significantly greater analytical capability, tolerance for short-term disruptions during change implementation, and the willingness to acknowledge fundamental process limitations rather than simply demanding greater effort within established approaches.

- **Anticipatory correction** is the most sophisticated pattern of adjustment, initiating modifications before performance gaps become apparent. These systems utilize early indicators, environmental monitoring, and predictive modeling to identify emerging issues while they remain manageable. They implement preventive measures designed to maintain goal alignment even in changing circumstances. This approach mitigates the performance degradation inherent in reactive methods. Still, it necessitates sophisticated prediction capabilities, a willingness to invest in addressing problems not yet fully manifested, and tolerance for occasional false positives that trigger unnecessary responses.

Most intricate systems incorporate multiple correction patterns tailored to different performance dimensions based on their characteristics. Critical safety variables may employ amplifying feedback to respond promptly to hazardous deviations. Stable operational processes might utilize negative feedback to maintain consistent performance with minimal disruptions. Strategic capabilities often benefit from learning-based approaches that drive fundamental improvement rather than merely stabilization. Novel or rapidly evolving areas may warrant anticipatory correction to prevent emerging issues from becoming entrenched problems.

Effective correction also necessitates appropriate response timing that aligns with the nature of the identified issues.

Some deviations necessitate immediate action to prevent escalation or irreversible consequences. Conversely, others benefit from deliberate assessment before response, ensuring that interventions address genuine issues rather than measurement artifacts or transitional fluctuations. The most complex situations may require staged responses, with immediate containment actions followed by more fundamental adjustments addressing root causes.

These correction patterns determine how effectively systems translate performance awareness into appropriate adjustments, maintaining goal alignment despite internal or external disruptions. Without effective correction mechanisms, even the most sensitive detection capabilities yield only awareness without improvement. Conversely, powerful correction methods only create value when guided by accurate detection that accurately identifies when and where adjustment is required.

Learning and Adaptation Mechanisms

Beyond immediate correction, sophisticated complex systems incorporate higher-order learning mechanisms that systematically enhance both detection and response capabilities through experience. These adaptation processes transform rudimentary feedback systems into continuously improving learning organizations:

- **Single-loop learning** represents the most fundamental adaptation process, gradually refining established methods based on performance outcomes. Systems identify which techniques yield superior results and progressively allocate resources toward more effective approaches. This evolutionary optimization operates within existing frameworks, enhancing efficiency and effectiveness without challenging fundamental assumptions. While generating reliable incremental improvements, single-loop learning remains constrained by existing mental models and operational paradigms, potentially optimizing outdated approaches rather than exploring transformative alternatives.

- **Double-loop learning** promotes more profound adaptation by critically examining underlying assumptions rather than refining techniques. When performance consistently falls short despite optimization efforts, double-loop processes scrutinize whether established goals, metrics, or mental models necessitate revision. This deeper learning facilitates paradigm shifts when existing frameworks prove inadequate for evolving circumstances or emerging challenges. While potentially more disruptive than single-loop approaches, double-loop learning provides essential renewal for systems undergoing fundamental change rather than merely incremental challenges.

- **Triple-loop learning** represents the most sophisticated adaptation, examining and improving the learning processes. Systems assess how effectively they detect, correct, and learn from experience, systematically enhancing their adaptation capabilities. This meta-learning creates progressively more intelligent organizations capable of faster, more effective responses to novel situations. Triple-loop learning proves particularly valuable for systems operating in rapidly changing environments where adaptation capability represents a critical success factor.

Effective learning systems balance exploration and exploitation across various adaptation levels.

Exploitation prioritizes refining existing approaches to achieve maximum efficiency and extracting the full potential of established knowledge. Conversely, exploration investigates novel approaches that may offer breakthrough improvements but entail greater uncertainty. This balance is dynamically adjusted based on environmental stability, performance adequacy, and available resources. In stable environments with incremental challenges, exploitation is emphasized. Conversely, a greater investment in exploration is warranted in turbulent conditions or performance crises.

Several organizational capabilities enable effective adaptation regardless of the specific learning approach. Knowledge management systems capture insights from experience, preventing lessons from being lost through personnel changes or memory limitations. Psychological safety creates environments where participants willingly acknowledge problems and propose novel solutions without fear of blame or ridicule. Experimental mindsets value learning from controlled failures as essential for discovering superior approaches. Reflection practices create deliberate space for thoughtful analysis rather than perpetual reactivity.

These learning mechanisms transform correction from repeated firefighting into progressive capability enhancement. They enable systems to address not merely today's performance gaps but tomorrow's emerging challenges. Perhaps most importantly, they create anti-fragile organizations that grow stronger through disruption rather than merely surviving it, converting problems into developmental opportunities rather than mere threats requiring minimization.

Defining Performance Metrics

Effective goal pursuit necessitates translating abstract objectives into tangible, quantifiable indicators that serve as tracking mechanisms for progress. Well-crafted performance metrics serve as focal points, direct resource allocation, and provide invaluable feedback for continuous improvement. Their design significantly shapes the areas of performance that receive attention and those that remain overlooked.

> *Performance metrics serve as communication devices that translate abstract goals into observable measures.*

Their design should adhere to several fundamental principles to effectively guide system behavior toward desired objectives:

- **Strategic alignment** is the most fundamental principle, ensuring metrics directly connect to priority goals. Each indicator should clearly advance specific objectives within the goal hierarchy, creating visible links between measurement activities and ultimate system purposes. This alignment prevents the common dysfunction where organizations measure what is easily quantifiable rather than what is genuinely important. It requires regular reassessment as goals evolve, preventing legacy metrics from driving continued attention to outdated priorities.

- **Balanced coverage** provides another essential principle, ensuring metrics collectively address all critical goal dimensions. Financial measures capture resource stewardship but typically miss quality, innovation, or long-term investment dimensions. Efficiency indicators track resource utilization but often overlook effectiveness in achieving ultimate outcomes. Output measures document production volume but frequently miss impact considerations determining whether outputs actually create the desired change. Comprehensive measurement frameworks incorporate multiple perspectives, preventing narrow optimization that advances measured dimensions at the expense of unmeasured dimensions.

- **Appropriate precision** balances measurement accuracy against practical constraints. Some performance dimensions justify sophisticated measurement with high precision, particularly where small variations significantly impact outcomes or where precise data collection costs are minimal. Others require only approximate indicators that capture directional performance without excessive investment in perfect measurement. Effective systems align precision with importance and measurement difficulty, preventing both sloppy approximation where precision is critical and excessive measurement burden where rough indicators suffice.

- **Controllability** represents a more contentious principle, focusing on whether measured entities can significantly influence results through their actions. Purely outcome-focused metrics, such as ultimate health status, may align perfectly with goals but depend substantially on factors beyond the control of healthcare providers. Process measures, such as preventive screening rates, offer greater controllability but a more distant connection to ultimate objectives. The most sophisticated approaches employ contribution analysis to identify which outcome elements respond to system actions, thereby creating controllability without abandoning outcome focus.

- **Resistance to gaming** recognizes that measurement influences behavior, sometimes creating perverse incentives that undermine genuine improvement. Narrow metrics often produce "hitting the target but missing the point" behaviors that optimize measured dimensions while sacrificing unmeasured aspects. Gaming-resistant designs employ several strategies: multiple complementary metrics preventing narrow optimization, balancing quantitative measures with qualitative assessment, shifting measurement focus to prevent adaptation to specific indicators, and creating holistic evaluation systems that consider contextual factors rather than mechanistic target comparison.

These design principles guide the development of metrics that genuinely advance system purposes rather than merely creating measurement activity. They transform performance tracking from disconnected monitoring into strategic tools that focus attention, guide resource allocation, and drive continuous improvement toward priority objectives.

Cascading Measurement Frameworks

Complex systems necessitate measurement methodologies that connect high-level objectives and specific operational activities while maintaining a cohesive focus across multiple organizational levels. Cascading measurement frameworks facilitate these connections, translating abstract objectives into concrete indicators pertinent to various system components:

- At the highest level, **outcome metrics** assess ultimate goal achievement—the fundamental impacts that justify system existence. Healthcare systems measure population health status, educational systems track student achievement and life outcomes, and economic systems monitor prosperity and resource distribution. These high-level indicators provide crucial feedback regarding whether the system fulfills its purpose. Still, they typically respond gradually to interventions and are influenced by numerous factors beyond the control of any specific subgroup.

- **Intermediate outcome metrics** establish bridges between ultimate objectives and specific activities by measuring precursors with established connections to final outcomes. Healthcare systems, for instance, track intermediate indicators such as blood pressure control, vaccination rates, or early detection percentages that predict ultimate health outcomes. Educational systems monitor engagement levels, skill development milestones, and knowledge acquisition that presage future achievement. These bridging metrics respond more swiftly to interventions while maintaining a clear relationship to ultimate goals, creating more actionable feedback loops that align with fundamental purposes.

- **Process metrics** are designed to monitor specific activities with established or theoretical connections to desired outcomes. These indicators assess whether systems effectively implement approaches believed to advance objectives. For instance, they evaluate whether healthcare providers adhere to evidence-based protocols, teachers utilize effective instructional methods, and financial advisors conduct appropriate client assessments. Process metrics provide highly actionable feedback with clear controllability. Still, their effectiveness depends on a comprehensive understanding of the process-outcome relationships to ensure genuine improvement rather than merely procedural compliance.

- **Input metrics** assess whether systems receive the necessary resources for effective performance. These measures evaluate financial resources, personnel qualifications, technology infrastructure, and other foundational elements required for successful operation. While not directly related to ultimate outcomes, input metrics provide essential context for interpreting other indicators. They help distinguish between performance issues stemming from implementation problems and resource inadequacy.

- **Effective measurement systems** integrate diverse metric types into coherent frameworks that establish clear connections between specific activities and their ultimate objectives. Strategy maps visually represent these relationships, illustrating how operational processes drive intermediate outcomes that ultimately advance strategic objectives. Balanced scorecards and similar approaches ensure appropriate attention to multiple dimensions—financial sustainability, customer experience, operational excellence, and capability development—preventing narrow optimization that prioritizes certain objectives at the expense of others.

These frameworks enable different system levels to concentrate on metrics most pertinent to their specific responsibilities while aligning with overall objectives. Executive leadership focuses on outcome metrics demonstrating strategic goal achievement. Middle management concentrates on intermediate indicators indicating progress toward outcomes. Operational staff attend to process metrics guiding daily activities. This division of measurement focus facilitates appropriate specialization while maintaining coherent direction through explicit linkage between metrics at different levels.

Cascading frameworks transform measurement from isolated activities into integrated systems that translate abstract purposes into concrete indicators without compromising strategic focus. They empower every system participant to comprehend how their responsibilities align with ultimate goals, establishing a clear connection between daily activities and fundamental purposes that imbues measurement with a deeper meaning beyond mere performance monitoring.

Dashboard and Visualization Techniques

Performance data holds value only when transformed into actionable insights that guide decision-making and foster improvement. Visualization techniques convert raw metrics into intuitive displays that reveal patterns, highlight critical issues, and support effective response:

- **Strategic dashboards** integrate key indicators into unified displays that showcase overall goal progress. These high-level visualizations prioritize outcome and strategic metrics while filtering operational details irrelevant to leadership focus. Effective strategic dashboards balance comprehensiveness and clarity, covering all critical objectives without overwhelming leaders with excessive information. They highlight exceptional conditions that require attention while providing the context necessary for appropriate interpretation. The most advanced approaches incorporate predictive elements that demonstrate projected performance trajectories alongside current status, enabling proactive response to emerging issues before they fully develop.

- **Operational dashboards** offer more detailed and frequently updated visualizations for managing day-to-day activities. These visualizations prioritize process and intermediate outcome metrics directly influencing current operations. They typically refresh more frequently than strategic dashboards, sometimes providing real-time data for time-sensitive processes. Effective operational dashboards effectively highlight immediate action priorities, often utilizing color coding, threshold indicators, or explicit alerting to identify issues requiring attention. They provide sufficient context for root cause identification while maintaining focus on metrics within operational control.

Both dashboard types benefit from several visualization principles that enhance insight generation. Comparative context transforms isolated numbers into meaningful evaluations by showing relevant benchmarks—historical trends, peer performance, established standards, or strategic targets. Appropriate granularity provides the necessary detail for action without overwhelming with excessive specificity, often through drill-down capabilities that reveal additional information on demand. Visual hierarchy directs attention to the most important information through size, position, color, and other design elements that create natural focus on priority indicators.

In addition to conventional dashboards, specialized visualization techniques cater to specific analytical requirements. Relationship visualizations elucidate connections between various metrics, uncovering correlations, causal chains, and interaction effects concealed in isolated indicators. Temporal visualizations illuminate patterns over time—trends, cycles, and anomalies—that remain obscured in static snapshots. Comparative visualizations juxtapose performance across diverse organizational units, exposing variations that may indicate either issues demanding attention or exemplary practices deserving dissemination.

Advanced approaches extend beyond passive display to interactive analysis tools that empower users to explore performance dynamics.

Filtering capabilities facilitate the examination of specific subgroups or conditions to identify differential performance patterns. Scenario modeling enables the exploration of how metric relationships might respond to potential interventions. Drill-down functionality permits progressive exploration from high-level patterns to underlying details when further investigation is warranted.

Effective visualization transforms performance measurement from data collection into insight generation that drives improvement. It converts abstract numbers into an intuitive understanding that supports better decisions at all system levels. Perhaps most importantly, it democratizes data access, enabling all system participants to comprehend performance patterns rather than restricting insights to analytical specialists with advanced statistical training.

Case Study: Goal Alignment in Healthcare Systems

To illustrate the practical application of unified goal analysis, let us analyze a case study involving the alignment of goals within a regional healthcare system. This case study demonstrates how decomposing overall goals, evaluating the contributions of subgroups, measuring alignment, analyzing feedback mechanisms, and designing performance metrics can provide practical insights that enhance system effectiveness.

Background and Challenge

The case concerned a mid-sized healthcare system comprising five hospitals, thirty ambulatory clinics, and various specialized services that served approximately 800,000 people across a diverse metropolitan region. Like many healthcare organizations, the system faced numerous competing pressures: delivering high-quality care, controlling rapidly escalating costs, addressing health disparities across population segments, maintaining financial sustainability, and adapting to emerging value-based payment models prioritizing outcomes over service volume.

Initial assessment revealed substantial goal confusion and misalignment. Different organizational units prioritized conflicting priorities, with some emphasizing clinical excellence irrespective of cost, others prioritizing financial performance over other considerations, and still others emphasizing patient satisfaction at times in conflict with clinical best practices. This misalignment resulted in inconsistent patient experiences, inefficient resource utilization, and suboptimal outcomes across multiple dimensions.

Leadership recognized that addressing these challenges necessitated more than merely issuing clarifications or stronger directives. The fundamental issue lay in systemic goal structures that inadvertently created conflicting incentives and unclear priorities. This realization prompted a comprehensive goal analysis initiative to establish greater alignment between individual, unit, and system-level objectives.

Goal Decomposition Process

The initiative commenced with a systematic analysis of how the system's ultimate objective—enhancing population health—decomposed into supporting objectives at various organizational levels. This analysis integrated multiple information sources: formal strategic documents, operational plans, budgetary allocations, performance metrics, and extensive stakeholder interviews with providers, administrators, staff, and patients.

The resulting goal hierarchy unveiled both anticipated and unexpected patterns. The anticipated framework encompassed conventional healthcare objectives, such as clinical quality, patient experience, financial sustainability, and population health. However, the analysis revealed substantial variations in how different stakeholders interpreted these broad categories and prioritized their components. Clinical quality, for instance, held distinct meanings for specialists focused on technical proficiency versus primary care providers emphasizing comprehensive well-being. Similarly, patient experience exhibited dramatically different interpretations across stakeholder groups, ranging from satisfaction with amenities to involvement in decision-making and minimizing unnecessary burdens.

Interdependency mapping further elucidated the relationship between these objectives, revealing both synergies and tensions. Some relationships exhibited natural alignment—evidence-based preventive care simultaneously enhanced clinical outcomes, improved patient experience, reduced long-term costs, and advanced population health. Conversely, other relationships highlighted fundamental tensions, particularly between short-term financial performance and investments in long-term population health improvements whose benefits may not be realized for several years.

Temporal goal analysis provided another crucial dimension by examining how objectives had evolved over time and the potential for future shifts. Historical analysis revealed a gradual transition from volume-oriented goals emphasizing service quantity toward value-oriented objectives prioritizing outcome quality. Environmental scanning suggested that this evolution would accelerate as payment models increasingly shifted financial risk to providers, necessitating greater emphasis on prevention, coordination, and long-term outcome management rather than discrete service delivery.

This decomposition process transformed abstract mission statements into concrete, actionable objectives with clear relationships.

It established a shared reference framework for subsequent alignment assessments, fostering a common language and explicit prioritization. This approach rendered misalignment discussions substantive rather than merely semantic or political.

Alignment Assessment Results

With a well-defined objective framework in place, the initiative systematically evaluated the alignment between individual incentives, unit objectives, and system-level goals. This assessment employed a comprehensive approach, including incentive structure analysis, behavioral observation, survey and interview data, and performance pattern examination.

The assessment uncovered several notable misalignment patterns. Financial incentive structures predominantly rewarded service volume rather than outcome value, potentially creating tension with quality and efficiency objectives. Professional incentives emphasized specialized excellence over system integration, sometimes leading to "clinical perfection at any cost" approaches that deviated from value-based models. Operational metrics are predominantly focused on departmental efficiency rather than cross-functional coordination, potentially undermining integrated care delivery. Cultural norms in many units prioritized provider convenience over patient-centered approaches, despite official rhetoric emphasizing the latter.

A comprehensive analysis of performance data utilizing machine learning techniques yielded invaluable insights by elucidating the specific behaviors that most effectively predicted the attainment of ultimate outcomes. This analysis revealed that coordination activities were frequently overlooked and undervalued within formal systems, exhibiting a strong correlation with clinical outcomes and cost efficiency. Conversely, certain activities that received substantial incentives demonstrated surprisingly weak relationships to priority outcomes when controlling for other variables, indicating potential misallocation of rewards and recognition.

A comprehensive feedback loop analysis was conducted to elucidate how the system detected and responded to misalignment, uncovering several concerning patterns. Delayed feedback resulted in situations where providers received performance information insufficiently timely for effective course correction. Fragmented feedback provided disparate organizational units with incomplete performance data, hindering systemic comprehension. In some instances, overwhelming feedback generated an excessive number of competing metrics, rendering prioritization an insurmountable challenge, despite the availability of abundant data. The assessment also revealed substantial variation in alignment across different system segments. Certain innovative units had developed locally-aligned structures with a clear correlation between individual incentives and collective outcomes. These "bright spots" provided valuable models for potential system-wide approaches, demonstrating practical alignment mechanisms already operational within the broader organization's context and constraints.

This thorough assessment transformed vague dissatisfaction with organizational performance into a precise understanding of the specific areas and mechanisms of misalignment.

It identified actionable intervention opportunities that would enhance goal harmony without necessitating unrealistic cultural transformations or substantial financial reorganizations beyond the authority of leadership.

Intervention Design and Implementation

Based on the alignment assessment, leadership developed a comprehensive intervention strategy addressing critical misalignment points. Instead of thoroughly reorganizing, the approach prioritized strategic adjustments to the most influential alignment mechanisms.

Performance metric redesign established a more equitable measurement framework that connects daily activities to ultimate outcomes. The new system utilizes cascading metrics, linking unit-specific indicators to system-level goals through explicit causal chains. This approach balances outcome measures, demonstrating ultimate impact, and process metrics providing actionable guidance. It incorporates financial and clinical perspectives, ensuring neither domain dominates decision-making. Furthermore, it significantly simplifies the previous metric proliferation, focusing attention on fewer high-impact indicators rather than overwhelming with excessive measurement.

Incentive restructuring modified both formal and informal rewards to better align with organizational priorities. Financial incentives shifted partially from volume to value, with compensation incorporating quality and efficiency components alongside productivity measures. Recognition systems elevated previously undervalued coordination and system-thinking behaviors. Career advancement pathways incorporated cross-functional experience and collaborative capability rather than solely specialized expertise. These adjustments maintained sufficient continuity to prevent disruptive transitions while introducing meaningful alignment improvements.

Feedback enhancement improved the flow of performance information throughout the organization. Integrated dashboards provided a unified performance perspective rather than fragmented metric collections. Predictive analytics identified potential issues before they fully manifested, enabling preventive rather than merely reactive responses. Cross-functional performance dialogues created a shared understanding of how different units' activities affected collective outcomes. These improvements transformed performance information from retrospective evaluation into prospective guidance that actually influenced decisions.

Structural adjustments modified organizational boundaries and authority relationships to better support aligned activities. Care delivery reorganized around patient populations rather than solely clinical specialties, creating natural alignment between provider success and patient outcomes. Decision rights shifted toward positions with broader system perspectives for issues with significant cross-functional impact. Resource allocation processes incorporated explicit goal alignment assessment in prioritization decisions. These structural changes created an organizational architecture that more naturally supports desired behaviors.

The implementation followed a deliberate sequence designed to build momentum while managing disruption. The initial focus on performance measurement and feedback systems created a clearer direction and provided better information before significant incentive changes raised accountability stakes. Limited pilots tested approaches before system-wide implementation, creating both evidence of effectiveness and practical examples others could observe. Extensive communication connected changes to the underlying purpose, ensuring participants understood why new approaches deserved support rather than merely what new requirements existed.

Outcomes and Lessons

Implementing the goal alignment initiative over its three-year duration yielded several notable outcomes. Clinical quality metrics demonstrated a 15-23% improvement across priority conditions, with particularly significant gains in areas necessitating cross-functional collaboration. Patient experience scores exhibited an overall increase of 18%, with the most substantial improvement observed in previously challenging care transitions. Per-capita cost trends declined from 5.8% annual growth to 3.2%, significantly surpassing regional comparison groups. Staff engagement metrics improved by 14%, reversing previous downward trends and mitigating costly turnover.

Beyond these quantitative results, several qualitative changes signaled a deeper improvement in alignment. Cross-functional collaboration increased spontaneously, as participants recognized the mutual benefits of coordinated approaches. Innovation efforts increasingly focus on high-priority system challenges rather than isolated local improvements. Difficult trade-off discussions became more substantive and solution-oriented, rather than devolving into territorial protection. These cultural shifts suggested that alignment improvement had become self-reinforcing rather than merely compliance driven.

The initiative also yielded several valuable lessons with broader application beyond this specific case. First, it demonstrated that meaningful alignment improvement does not necessitate complete organizational transformation or perfect incentive design. Strategic adjustments to the most impactful mechanisms can create substantial progress within practical constraints. Second, it emphasized the importance of addressing multiple alignment dimensions simultaneously—metrics, incentives, feedback, and structure—rather than expecting any single mechanism to achieve comprehensive alignment. Third, it revealed the value of explicitly mapping goal relationships and interdependencies before attempting alignment improvement, thereby preventing simplistic approaches that might inadvertently create unintended consequences by overlooking complex objective interactions.

Perhaps most importantly, the case illustrates how goal alignment represents a dynamic, ongoing process rather than a static end state. As healthcare continued evolving toward value-based models, population health management, and greater digitization, alignment mechanisms required continuous adjustment to maintain synchronization between individual incentives and emerging collective purposes. This perspective shifted the organizational focus from seeking permanent alignment solutions to building adaptive capabilities that could maintain alignment through ongoing environmental and strategic evolution.

Conclusion

Unified Goal Analysis provides crucial insights into how intricate systems, comprising independent actors, pursue collective objectives. By systematically analyzing how overall goals are decomposed into manageable components, how various subgroups contribute to goal achievement, how individual incentives align with collective objectives, how feedback mechanisms maintain goal direction, and how performance metrics track progress, this approach elucidates fundamental drivers of system behavior.

The methodologies elucidated in this chapter transform abstract discussions of purpose and values into tangible, actionable understanding of goal structures and relationships. Goal decomposition explicitly reveals how ultimate purposes translate into specific objectives at different system levels. Subgroup contribution analysis elucidates how different components advance collective purposes through complementary functions. Alignment assessment identifies where individual incentives support or undermine system goals. Feedback loop analysis examines how systems detect and rectify performance deviations. Performance metric design creates measurement approaches focusing on priority objectives while preventing narrow optimization.

These analytical approaches provide valuable guidance for system improvement efforts. They identify specific misalignment points where intervention would enhance goal harmony without necessitating comprehensive reorganization. They reveal feedback weaknesses that prevent effective self-correction despite good intentions. They expose measurement gaps or distortions that divert attention from core purposes toward secondary concerns. Perhaps most importantly, they establish a connection between daily operational activities and ultimate system purposes, enabling participants to comprehend how their specific contributions contribute to meaningful collective objectives.

In the subsequent chapter, we will construct upon this goal-oriented foundation to explore iterative refinement and validation methodologies. These approaches continuously enhance our comprehension of intricate systems through systematic testing against empirical reality, ensuring that our models, analyses, and interventions remain grounded in practical effectiveness rather than theoretical elegance.

CHAPTER 11

Iterative Refinement and Validation

T he fundamental challenge in modeling hidden networks lies not in creating the initial model, but in the rigorous, continuous process of refinement that follows. As we have explored throughout this book, complex systems composed of independent actors create emergent behaviors that often defy simplistic analysis. The greatest insights come not from static snapshots, but from dynamic validation processes that mirror the adaptive nature of these networks themselves.

Model Validation Against Real-World Data

No model of intricate, concealed networks can be regarded as reliable without a comprehensive validation process against empirical data. This validation procedure must transcend mere correlation analysis to establish causal relationships between model predictions and actual outcomes. One particularly effective approach involves counterfactual testing, examining what the model predicts would transpire under conditions that did not occur, subsequently comparing these predictions with analogous historical scenarios.

The Global Financial Crisis of 2008 serves as an illustrative example. Numerous pre-crisis models failed to discern the systemic risks emerging from the mortgage-backed securities market because they were validated solely against the recent historical data, a period characterized by escalating housing prices and low default rates. The models lacked counterfactual validation against scenarios involving substantial housing market corrections. The shortcomings become evident when we retrospectively evaluate crisis-era models against historical housing market corrections from the 1980s and 1990s.

Effective validation necessitates the integration of diverse data sources that capture various facets of the concealed network.

In the context of terrorist network analysis, this encompasses communication metadata, financial transactions, travel patterns, and ideological content analysis. Each data stream offers a distinct perspective on the network, and convergent findings obtained across multiple streams substantially enhance validation. Conversely, divergence often indicates intriguing anomalies that warrant further investigation or model refinement.

Furthermore, the validation process should acknowledge the observer effect—the inherent tendency of observation to influence network behavior. When terrorist networks become aware of their communications being monitored, they exhibit adaptive responses. Similarly, tax evaders modify their strategies in response to tax authorities implementing novel detection algorithms. Consequently, validation should be regarded as an ongoing process rather than a singular certification.

Parameter Tuning and Optimization

The intricacy of hidden networks often necessitates models with a substantial number of parameters. Financial market models, for instance, may incorporate hundreds of variables, encompassing a wide range of factors such as macroeconomic indicators and individual investor psychology. Ecological models tracking invasive species might include parameters for reproduction rates, predator-prey interactions, and environmental constraints. The challenge lies in optimizing these parameters to maximize model accuracy while simultaneously avoiding overfitting.

Bayesian optimization approaches have demonstrated remarkable effectiveness in parameter tuning for hidden network models.

Unlike grid search methods that exhaustively explore every possible parameter combination, Bayesian optimization constructs a probability model of the objective function that maps parameters to validation accuracy. This enables intelligent exploration of the parameter space, directing computational resources towards promising regions.

Cross-validation techniques are indispensable in preventing overfitting during parameter tuning. k-fold cross-validation, where the data is partitioned into k subsets with each subset serving as validation data once while the remaining k-1 subsets serve as training data, ensures that the model generalizes beyond the specific data used for training. Temporal cross-validation, where models are trained on earlier time periods and validated on subsequent ones, holds particular significance for dynamic networks.

Ensemble methods, which combine multiple models with distinct parameters, frequently outperform any single optimized model. By aggregating predictions from diverse models, ensemble methods can capture various aspects of network behavior and mitigate the influence of individual model biases. In counterterrorism applications, ensemble approaches that integrate social network analysis, financial transaction monitoring, and communication pattern detection have demonstrated superior effectiveness compared to any single analytical approach.

Hypothesis Testing Methodologies

The scientific method provides a robust framework for refining concealed network models through hypothesis testing. This iterative process commences with the formulation of testable predictions based on the prevailing model, followed by the design of experiments or observational studies to validate these predictions. Subsequently, the results obtained are utilized to refine the model.

Agent-based simulations have emerged as a progressively favored methodology for hypothesis testing in concealed networks. By constructing virtual environments populated with autonomous agents adhering to predetermined rules, researchers can observe emergent behaviors and compare them to empirical patterns. Upon the identification of discrepancies, the underlying rules can be modified until simulation outputs converge with observed data.

In the realm of internet dark markets, researchers have employed agent-based simulations to investigate the formation of trust networks in the absence of centralized authority. By manipulating parameters pertaining to reputation systems, transaction verification, and information sharing, these simulations elucidate the mechanisms that most closely replicate the observed patterns in actual dark markets. The findings have challenged conventional assumptions regarding the indispensable role of trusted third parties in market systems.

Natural experiments where external events induce conditions akin to controlled experiments—offer another valuable hypothesis testing methodology. The closure of Silk Road, a prominent darknet marketplace, served as a natural experiment for testing hypotheses regarding the reorganization of hidden networks following significant disruptions. Analysis revealed that rather than dismantling the network, the shutdown catalyzed a more decentralized system with enhanced security protocols—an insight that substantially refined models of network resilience.

A/B testing methodologies, originating from the technology industry, have been adapted to assess hypotheses regarding concealed network interventions. By implementing slightly divergent policy approaches in comparable settings and evaluating outcomes, policymakers can empirically validate which interventions most effectively alter network behavior. Tax authorities have employed this approach to evaluate various communication strategies aimed at enhancing compliance among informal economy participants.

Continuous Monitoring Systems

The dynamic nature of hidden networks necessitates continuous monitoring rather than periodic assessments. Real-time monitoring systems that monitor key indicators and automatically flag significant deviations from anticipated patterns have become indispensable components of model validation and refinement.

Anomaly detection algorithms serve as the foundation of these monitoring systems. These algorithms establish baseline behavior patterns for the network and identify anomalous deviations. In financial systems, anomaly detection may identify unusual trading patterns that could indicate market manipulation. In epidemiological networks, it may identify unexpected patterns of symptom reporting that suggest emerging disease outbreaks.

The distinction between significant anomalies and statistical noise presents a significant challenge. Adaptive thresholding techniques, which adjust sensitivity based on context, have demonstrated effectiveness. For instance, financial transaction monitoring systems may apply more stringent anomaly thresholds during periods of market volatility, when unusual patterns are more likely to represent legitimate reactions to external events rather than illicit activity.

Federated monitoring systems, which share information across institutional boundaries while preserving privacy, have emerged as particularly powerful tools. In cybersecurity applications, these systems enable organizations to benefit from collective threat intelligence without exposing sensitive details about their internal networks. Similar approaches have been employed to track money laundering networks across financial institutions and jurisdictions.

The most sophisticated monitoring systems incorporate feedback loops that continuously enhance detection capabilities. When anomalies are flagged and subsequently investigated, the outcomes of those investigations are returned to the system, refining future anomaly detection. This establishes an evolutionary process where monitoring capabilities co-evolve with the networks they monitor.

Hidden networks do not exist in static environments. External factors, such as technological innovations, regulatory changes, social movements, and economic shifts, constantly reshape the landscape in which networks operate. Effective models must adapt to these changing environments or quickly become obsolete.

Dynamic Adaptation and Integration of New Technologies

The rapid pace of technological advancement presents both challenges and opportunities for modeling concealed networks. Emerging technologies such as artificial intelligence, quantum computing, blockchain, and advanced sensor networks fundamentally alter the operational dynamics and observation methods of hidden networks.

Dynamic adaptation necessitates models capable of integrating novel technological capabilities as they emerge. For instance, the integration of natural language processing and computer vision has revolutionized our ability to analyze terrorist propaganda networks, enabling automated systems to identify conceptual linkages and ideological evolution that would be inaccessible to manual tracking. Models that failed to incorporate these capabilities quickly became obsolete as the volume of online content surged exponentially.

Technological integration operates bidirectionally, with hidden networks rapidly adopting new technologies and often repurpose them in unexpected ways. Criminal networks have embraced encrypted messaging applications, cryptocurrency mixers, and location spoofing tools. Effective models must anticipate how emerging technologies might be deployed by the networks they track. Predictive frameworks that simulate how rational actors might leverage new technologies have proven valuable in staying ahead of adaptive network behaviors.

The ongoing "technological arms race" between researchers studying concealed networks and those operating within them necessitates continuous innovation in modeling methodologies. Federated learning techniques, for instance, now enable intelligence agencies to collaborate on enhancing threat detection models without sharing sensitive data, thereby overcoming previous jurisdictional limitations. Similarly, homomorphic encryption facilitates pattern analysis on encrypted data while preserving privacy, thereby revealing network structures.

Most importantly, effective adaptation necessitates interdisciplinary collaboration that bridges technological expertise with domain knowledge. When blockchain analytics tools were initially developed to monitor illicit cryptocurrency transactions, their primary focus was on technical transaction patterns. However, it was only when these tools were integrated with conventional financial intelligence methodologies that they achieved their true potential in identifying money laundering networks. This integration amalgamated technological capabilities with a profound comprehension of the modus operandi of financial criminals.

Transfer learning techniques have demonstrated efficacy in adapting models to novel environments. These approaches draw upon knowledge acquired in one context to enhance performance in another. For instance, models designed to monitor wildlife trafficking networks in Southeast Asia have been successfully adapted to African contexts by retaining general network principles while retraining specific parameters to account for regional variations.

Concept drift detection algorithms assist in identifying instances where environmental changes have diminished the effectiveness of existing models. These algorithms monitor the correlation between model inputs and outputs over time, identifying situations where previously established patterns no longer hold. In the context of financial compliance, such algorithms may detect instances where money laundering techniques have evolved to evade existing detection mechanisms.

Adversarial training techniques deliberately expose models to simulated evasion attempts, fortifying their resilience against adaptive network behaviors. By incorporating "red team" exercises where experts attempt to circumvent detection systems, these approaches anticipate the potential evolution of concealed networks in response to monitoring initiatives. Tax authorities have successfully employed adversarial training to enhance evasion detection systems by enlisting experienced auditors to design undetectable evasion strategies.

The most adaptable models incorporate self-modification mechanisms that automatically adapt to changing environments. Evolutionary algorithms that generate multiple model variations, evaluate their performance, and propagate successful variations have demonstrated promise in tracking rapidly evolving networks, such as online extremist communities that frequently relocate platforms and communication strategies.

Case Study: Evolving Financial Regulatory Systems

The global financial regulatory system serves as an illustrative case study in iterative refinement and validation of methodologies for detecting and mitigating hidden networks. Following the 2008 financial crisis, international regulators recognized that existing frameworks had inadequately captured systemic risk's intricate and interconnected nature within the financial system. This prompted a fundamental reevaluation of regulatory approaches.

The Bank for International Settlements' evolution of the Basel Accords exemplifies the iterative refinement process. Basel I (1988) established simple capital requirements primarily based on credit risk. Basel II (2004) expanded this framework to include operational and market risks, permitting banks to utilize internal models for risk assessment. When the financial crisis exposed the shortcomings of this approach, Basel III (2010) and subsequently Basel IV introduced more sophisticated requirements addressing liquidity risk, leverage, and systemic importance.

Each iteration represented a refinement based on observed failures in the preceding framework. The transition from Basel II to Basel III particularly exemplifies model validation against real-world data—the financial crisis served as the ultimate stress test, revealing which aspects of the regulatory model had failed to capture critical systemic risks.

The implementation of stress testing regimes by central banks worldwide underscores the paramount importance of hypothesis testing methodologies. These tests pose counterfactual scenarios, such as severe recessions, market crashes, and liquidity crises, and assess how financial institutions would perform under such conditions. The outcomes of these tests serve as both institution-specific requirements and system-wide regulatory approaches. Over time, the evolution of stress test scenarios reflects a continuous learning process, as it reveals which hypothetical conditions most effectively expose hidden vulnerabilities.

Developing transaction monitoring systems for anti-money laundering (AML) compliance exemplifies the challenges associated with parameter tuning and optimization. Early AML systems generated excessive false-positive alerts, leading to "compliance fatigue" and ironically facilitating the evasion of truly suspicious transactions. Through iterative refinement, these systems now incorporate machine learning algorithms that continuously optimize detection parameters based on investigation outcomes, significantly enhancing precision without compromising recall.

Perhaps most significantly, financial regulators have increasingly adopted continuous monitoring approaches rather than point-in-time examinations. For instance, the U.S. Office of the Comptroller of the Currency has shifted toward "continuous supervision" of large financial institutions, with examiners maintaining an ongoing presence rather than conducting periodic reviews. This reflects the recognition that financial risks emerge from dynamic network behaviors that cannot adequately assess through static snapshots.

The evolution continues as regulators adapt to the rise of fintech, cryptocurrency, and decentralized finance. Each innovation creates new hidden networks that require fresh modeling approaches. The regulatory response to these developments exemplifies adaptation to changing environments, with frameworks like regulatory sandboxes allowing for controlled experimentation with novel approaches.

This case study demonstrates that effective governance of hidden networks requires not just sophisticated initial models but commitment to the ongoing processes of validation, refinement, and adaptation. As the financial system continues to evolve, so too must the regulatory approaches designed to monitor and stabilize it.

Conclusion

The study of concealed networks, whether they facilitate terrorism, financial crime, disease transmission, or beneficial social movements, necessitates humility. Despite the sophistication of our models, they represent approximations of immensely complex systems. The quality of these approximations is contingent not upon their initial elegance but on our unwavering commitment to rigorous and ongoing refinement.

The technological landscape continues to evolve at an accelerating pace, with each innovation introducing novel capabilities and vulnerabilities within concealed networks. As quantum computing poses a threat to current encryption standards, as artificial general intelligence approaches reality, and as mixed reality environments blur the distinction between physical and digital interactions, the nature of concealed networks will undergo transformations beyond our current comprehension. Our modeling approaches must evolve not merely incrementally but transformative, integrating emerging technological paradigms as they emerge.

The methodologies outlined in this chapter—empirical validation, parameter optimization, hypothesis testing, continuous monitoring, and adaptive response—formulate a framework for this refinement process. By adopting these approaches, researchers and practitioners can construct models that not only elucidate the current state of hidden networks but also anticipate their evolution in the future.

As computational capabilities advance and data collection becomes more sophisticated, our ability to model hidden networks will undoubtedly improve. However, the fundamental challenges will persist: How do we validate models of systems that resist direct observation? How do we optimize parameters when ground truth remains elusive? How do we test hypotheses about networks that adapt to our very attempts to study them? And perhaps most importantly, how do we ensure that our models evolve as rapidly as the networks they attempt to capture?

The solutions lie not in any single methodology but in the iterative process itself. This process involves a commitment to continuous learning, testing, and refinement, which mirrors the adaptive nature of the networks we seek to understand. In this ongoing dialogue between model and reality, we find our best hope for illuminating the concealed networks that shape our world.

Index

www.ingramcontent.com/pod-product-compliance
Lightning Source LLC
Chambersburg PA
CBHW071542210326
41597CB00019B/3086